evelio's garden

Memoir of a Naturalist in Costa Rica

Other books by Sandra Shaw Homer:

Letters from the Pacific: 49 Days on a Cargo Ship

Journey to the Joie de Vivre:
Lessons to be Found on the Road (If We Look for Them)

The Magnificent Dr. Wao

evelio's garden

Memoir of a Naturalist in Costa Rica

Sandra Shaw Homer

atmosphere press

This one's for Mom

Table of Contents

The morning wind forever blows, the poem of creation is uninterrupted; but few are the ears that hear it.
-Henry David Thoreau

. . . il faut cultiver notre jardin.
-Voltaire

Prologue

They say the wind drives some people crazy. Evelio is certainly having trouble with it this year. It shoots through the funnel between the volcano and the hills, picking up speed as it races unobstructed the length of the lake, and rakes through his organic garden "burning" his beans.

It's no accident that the first wind towers in Costa Rica were built on the ridge – the Continental Divide – just behind our house. And our land, chosen for its spectacular view of Lake Arenal and three volcanoes, sits right in the teeth of it.

Common wisdom in Costa Rica is that if it's blowing, it's not raining, and vice versa. But here on the lake, that tropical two-season pattern no longer holds. The wind drives the rain horizontally, pounding the house like a freight train, seemingly at any time of year. The common wisdom, however, has been slow to catch up, and this has challenged Evelio, and his garden, to the point that he feels personally at war with the weather.

The wind has been churning up the past, certain memories I have buried for too long, as well as others that are helping me to put things in perspective. I have wanted to set some of this down for a long time. In my life here – twenty-nine years now – I have been buffeted by more than the Trade Winds; and as their pattern has changed, so have I.

One morning I felt a tectonic shift in my mental landscape. Presiding at a meeting of the Environmental Commission, I suddenly experienced an unbearable cacophony of Spanish voices around the table, and I could understand nothing. All I could hear was my thudding heart, and there wasn't enough air in the room. Overworked and overstressed, I had to drop all my environmental work and reassess.

It was late 2009 – a good time to look at how I had stood up to the gales my life in Costa Rica had been throwing at me. I needed to focus on small things, give myself time to reflect, write.

But how could I know that Evelio was going to take over the story?

October
Evelio vs. Nature, Round One

Evelio is really pissed at Fortuna. He stomped up to my office today and thrust a half-eaten cucumber through the open door. What can I do? The dogs have discovered the cucumbers, and Fortuna has no delicacy in her ravaging of the garden. She unearths an entire plant in order to drag off a juicy vegetable the perfect size and shape for gnawing.

Yesterday I walked fruitlessly the length of three 30-yard rows, bending down to lift up the broad leaves in search of what Fortuna finds using her nose alone. I have bopped her on that nose with her stolen goods and have shouted a firm "No!" twice now, but I have no hope she'll change her behavior. Evelio says old dogs are impossible – *malcriados* – misbehaved, untrainable.

"Evelio, she's a street dog," I say. "She grew up in town surviving any way she could, including raiding gardens and garbage cans."

But Evelio's fury is unabated. "Who ever heard of a dog that eats cucumbers!" shaking the offending vegetable in my direction.

"A starving dog, Evelio. And even though we feed her well, old habits die hard."

"But these are organic!"

I have to laugh at him. "And how is she to know *that*?" I am reminded of our friend Susanna, the biologist, who once told me to pinch Fortuna's lip (or bite it!) until she yelps, thus making myself the alpha dog around here. But even if I were, Fortuna would still be stealing cucumbers behind my back.

Although stealing cucumbers is a specialty, Fortuna does her greatest damage in the garden when she approaches it from the house at a flying run, bounding through all that delicate new greenery like a floppy-eared impala. It's fun to watch her soar like that, but when all four paws hit the tender vegetables, we all share the pain. So, to placate Evelio today, I offer to contribute financially to the fence he wants to build along the side of the garden facing the house. It won't keep Fortuna out, but it may reduce the damage. Since our investment in this project is likely to be well past the value of the few vegetables we'll eat, I have been resisting. But keeping Evelio happy seems to be part of my job around here.

Evelio is one of those people who are hard to shake. My husband, Roger, who has the kindness to adopt the less fortunate, found Evelio working as a night guard at a local windsurf center and decided he could teach Evelio how to finish drywall. He was very busy with construction projects at the time and wanted an assistant.

After his own projects were finished, Roger continued to find Evelio work, and in time his construction skills were honed to the point where he turned out to be a valuable member of the crew that built our new house. After that, he just hung around. A house, like a manuscript, is never really finished, and we had moved in long before all the details were done, so Evelio continued to make himself useful to the point where he became part of the furniture – just as Koki, our gardener and general factotum, and Rosa, our part-time house-keeper, have long been part of our daily lives.

One finds, at a certain age and living in a country where labor is relatively cheap, that washing windows and fixing barbed-wire fences are better left to younger, stronger hands. The price for this is a certain measure of privacy. Like Rosa, Evelio was walking into the house as if he owned it, no knocking, no calling *"Upe!"* Koki at least whistles for me to come to the door.

One day I came home from doing errands in town to receive the news from an excited Evelio that he was going to create an organic garden along the vacant stretch of our property facing the lake. This annoyed me. I could imagine that Evelio had presented Roger with the idea and my husband saying "Sure" without the faintest idea of what was being proposed. In any event, what happened to a former citrus orchard, a field Koki had persuaded Roger to denude to improve the view, wasn't important enough to mention. Beans don't grow as tall as orange trees.

My only conditions to this *fait accompli* were that the garden had to be 100 percent organic – absolutely no chemicals of any kind – and that we would like to eat some of his harvest in exchange for his use of our land. "And," I cautioned, "we don't have a lot of money to support this project, Evelio." He nodded vigorously, assuring me that the garden would pay for itself.

We live on a stretch of country road between two *quebradas*, among dozens of gullies and gorges carrying water from springs rising in the hills down to the basin of the lake. These remain as small patches of jungle threading through open fields and pasture. One of these *quebradas* runs alongside the original house on the property, deeply green and jungly, and filled in their seasons with toucans, *oropéndolas*, bejeweled hummingbirds, chattering parrots. Howler monkeys roam up and down the *quebrada* in search of tender new leaves, roaring everybody awake within miles precisely at dawn. There are other creatures not so visible, nor so welcome. Opossums, coatis, kinkajous, skunks, tayras, weasels, squirrels, and porcupines – some of these have squeezed into the bodega at night to steal the bananas ripening there. There were iguanas in the roof, scorpions in the closet. Once, two baby armadillos scooted out of the woods to frolic on the grass near Roger, who was working on his car, brushing right past his legs.

We built the new house high on a promontory overlooking the lake and volcanoes Arenal, Tenorio and Miravalles in the north central highlands. We had lived in the little house on the property for six years, dreaming this home and talking it over in endless detail, before an inheritance finally allowed us to build it. It's a traditional tropical house with a twist – two stories high – with deep overhanging roofs, a wraparound verandah, high ceilings, and beautiful teak woodwork (Roger's specialty). We live on the second floor to take advantage of the view, while Roger's workshop and office, along with the garage and laundry, are down below. This may not have been the greatest idea, because "down below" is where my husband spends most of his time, but at least the noise and sawdust are contained.

My space is above, in an office filled with beautiful things, where I can work on my writing and teach my occasional gringo Spanish students undisturbed. After living in cramped quarters for so long, it was a relief to find ourselves in such a light, airy, open and beautiful space. "Do we really live here?" Roger asked the day after the move.

The first fuzzy green beans hang hidden under their

leafy plants, and they are exactly the same green as the red-lored parrots that came through here last weekend, hundreds of them, all gabbling excitedly in the two *madero negro* trees behind the rock garden. When they take over a tree, the entire foliage *vibrates*. And while they are virtually invisible due to their perfect camouflage, it's hard to guess what benefit that serves birds whose raucous, non-stop, shrieking conversations so clearly give them away. There is no fruit on the *madero negro* trees (I walked out there and looked), so I have no explanation for why those parrots were there. They just took over those two trees for a noisy social hour and then flew off in huge beating flocks, screaming away down the wind.

My friend Irene, who's lived most of her life in New York, came by this afternoon while I was in the kitchen and told me she had never tasted a green bean just picked that afternoon and cooked for dinner. I find this amazing. We didn't have vegetable gardens when I was growing up, but we lived in rural Pennsylvania, where such riches as fresh green beans, ripe tomatoes and sweet corn were everywhere. I helped snap beans, shell peas, and shuck corn on my friends' front porches while they were still sun-warm in my hands. These beans in Evelio's garden are rich reminders of the northern summers of childhood, timeless and memory-perfect.

Not yet fifty, Evelio is the oldest of eight brothers, only one of whom has married. He's a compact, stocky man who speaks in such short, rapid-fire bursts that I have a hard time understanding him. When you speak to him, he cocks his head and turns one ear toward you, as if he were deaf in the other, so that, between his incapacities and mine, conversations are a challenge at best. I always have to ask clarifying questions – a good strategy when trying to understand another language anyway.

We have met most of Evelio's brothers over the years: among them, Carlito with his terrible stutter, who still lives at home with his mother; Flaco (a nickname that means skinny), who has wandered for years from job to job – including in Montreal – and has an incredible talent for picking up languages (English, French and German); and Cristhian, who also speaks English and worked at a local windsurf center in more prosperous days, then dabbled in real estate long enough to make one big commission, spent it immediately on a used car, and is now helping to grow beans on his father's farm.

Most of them have displayed an entrepreneurial streak of one kind or another, but few of these ventures endure. Maybe a lack of skills – I don't think any of them has made it through high school – but also there seems to be something in the family psyche, a wandering spirit or perhaps a lack of focus. There's something about the whole clan that's a little out of touch with this world. Maybe it's the discombobulations of moving into the twenty-first century directly from the nineteenth – something this whole rural culture shares. But there's a little more to it in Evelio's case: he actively *resists* change, and his stubborn impatience doesn't serve him well. As I come to know him better, I realize that this garden adventure is going to involve me in a constant effort to keep him on track.

The garden has been Evelio's opportunity to return to working the land he loves. Unfortunately, this means daily appearances: Farmer Evelio rides over here on his Chinese-built-always-breaking-down mountain bike, wearing his biking tights and helmet, changes into his farming clothes in the woodshed (now the garden shed), grabs his hoe and shovel and sets to work. We see him out there, dark curly head bent over his beans, muscular arms pulling tirelessly at his hoe, and we are impressed by his energy and dedication.

But we learned long ago that Costa Ricans are happier working together than alone, so Evelio ignores our desire for privacy every time he wants a little reinforcement for whatever he's doing – letting us know he's taking the wheelbarrow across the road to fetch horse manure to feed his compost-producing California red worms, borrowing my blender to mix his stinky pesticide, enlisting emergency help in bagging green beans to sell at the nearby hotel on gringo nights, asking us to pick up rice hulls from the nursery on our next trip into town. He wants our almost daily involvement in this project, and I'm struggling to remain calm.

It would be better if he had thought all this through before he started, but the garden has been driven by his fantasies right from the beginning: that he would revolutionize agriculture around the lake; that he would attract the interest and helping hands of others who would want to participate in the project; that he would find a ready market for everything he grew. When reality bites, he slides into a funk and needs a heavy dose of emotional support to keep him going.

At the beginning of every encounter with him, I try to remember to take a deep breath. I try to remember to focus on the moment, to listen to what's really going on inside him. I try to remember that, in giving him my present attention, I am not losing anything, but rather gaining by the exercise of my compassion. These things do not come naturally to me. My old life was lived in the Fast Lane, and I thought that was a good thing. It took years living in Costa Rica for me to begin to figure out that there's a higher mortality rate in that lane, and that there's a lot we speedsters are missing. "Why are you always in such a hurry?" Baptist pastor-cum-dent-fixer Franklin asked me once when I dashed into his body shop to find out when my father's car would be ready. "Because I want to get where I'm going," I laughed, not at all getting the point.

Others have written eloquently about the value of the journey over the destination, but I never understood this until I had lived a long time in a place where my need to get-there-in-a-hurry proved so dysfunctional.

In Costa Rica, it's not only about the value of stopping to smell the roses along the way; life has more to do with relating to others and an abiding sense of courtesy, both of which, of course, take time.

I came to Costa Rica with my ex-husband in 1990, in the hope of finding a kinder lifestyle, a warmer climate, and the opportunity to do those things we really enjoyed. He wanted to garden and fish and be in the outdoors; I wanted to start seriously writing for myself, instead of for others.

Some people adapt easily to other cultures. My mother imbued in me a love of travel and the sense that learning another language opened a door to a whole new, exciting, and possibly beautiful world. Although it took a while for me to learn how to create my days outside the confines of a full-time job, I found everything around me so interesting – the people, the daily life in the little village where we lived, the challenges of farm life and cooking what grew all around us, and, of course, the language – that I soon felt my new life had launched and my horizons were expanding.

My husband, on the other hand, terribly missed the stature he had enjoyed in his profession in Philadelphia, and he began to feel somehow lessened by this move we had made. Always a heavy drinker, within a year he had fallen into a bottle of vodka, and he never came up for air. I can't apologize to myself any more for my failures in that marriage – I'm sure I handled a lot of it badly. But, finally, I knew I couldn't try anymore, and I had to release myself from his life and start again to create my own. Six years after we arrived in Costa Rica, I left him.

We had begun near Grecia, in a house on a hill with a long view of the mountains to the south. Up to that moment, my adult life had been spent in cities – in tiny apartments, cramped row houses, office cubicles, and narrow streets with no sky above them. Costa Rica suddenly brought me back to a part of myself I had forgotten, my country childhood, and I felt a great emptiness starting to fill up. When in 1994 we moved to Lake Arenal to be closer to the fishing, the house was smaller and the view shrank, but almost anywhere around the lake one could take a deep breath and feel enriched by the beauty. I gave up on the short stories I was trying to write and began to write about what was around me: not only the natural world, but the people and the culture. Encouraged by writer friends, I landed a regular column in *The Tico Times*. I didn't know it at the time, but I was rushing toward my independence.

Alcoholics are emotional abusers – they can't help it, it's all they know. They pull you into their vortex and make you feel responsible for everything that's wrong, especially their illness. So you try rescue after rescue, which inevitably fail, and the failures mount up so high that it's impossible to feel good about yourself, about anything. To rescue my own sinking soul, I had to break away. Writing was my way out.

Entering another world is easy for me: I let my self go and open my eyes and heart and fall into it. And since I know I'm probably going to write about it later, I pay attention to the details. Perhaps writers suck up life from the things around them. Is this a form of theft? Do we plagiarize the living in order to feel alive ourselves?

I fell into the world Evelio grew up in when my Spanish teacher, Rosa Emilia, invited me on an *excursión*. She provided no details except that her uncle Francisco was leading. It was a typical family outing – complete with coolers, kids, and camp chairs – up into the dusty hills north of Cañas, to a remote farm with an unpainted wooden house shaded by an enormous *guanacaste* tree. There were no vehicles, no electric wires, no telephone poles. The family, a mother and three grown sons, greeted each of us with the traditional kiss on the cheek. The sons wore no socks in their misshapen leather shoes. The mother's hair, in the style of country women of a certain generation, was wound elaborately around her head with a pompadour perched on top. They were delighted to see us, even with no advance notice of our coming. Rosa Emilia whispered that Francisco had met the family when he taught school in the district many years before. I imagined these rangy sons with their pant legs above their ankles squeezing under child-sized desks in a one-room schoolhouse with the horses parked out front. Francisco had arrived at school every day on horseback, too.

14

The brothers led us across a wide savannah to a patch of dry tropical forest. There had been no rain in many months, and sky and earth were the same pale tawny color. It was perfect rattlesnake country, and I was glad I was on one of the two horses. Eventually, we picked our way down a steep little gorge to a river, and we used the horses to ferry everyone across. A short hike beyond the river was a lichened wall of petroglyphs: six yards high and 15 long, covered with pre-Columbian carvings of monkeys, fish, iguanas, humans, suns, moons, snakes, unfathomable geometric shapes – a fantasy in stone.

There are ancient places – I have only encountered a few of these in my life – that give one an extraordinary sense of suddenly being stretched back in time. At these moments, I feel the innocent heart of some much earlier person peeking through my eyes at the marvel in front of me.

Back at the farmhouse, the *señora* served a simple stew of root vegetables, onions, and small bits of meat. I furtively asked Rosa Emilia what the meat was, and she said it was beef that had been dried in the sun. It was tough but tasty. I leaned back from the table against the shiny boards of the farmhouse wall as Francisco serenaded us on his out-of-tune guitar. The carpentry of those boards cut so many years ago had been perfect, the walls still seamless, the planks straight and true. I was sure the trees had been felled on this same farm, the boards cut and planed by hand and worn smooth by many generations.

To me, the life on that farm was familiar only from movies, but to Evelio, who grew up that way, it is as familiar as the face of his grandfather. I need to remember this before making any assumptions about a shared culture. It's not only language that separates Evelio and me, but time.

October rains. This is the time of year when earth on sloping ground, saturated with water, begins to let go. Little piles of mud and grass start appearing in the drainage ditches along the road into town. Then bigger piles of mud that the town has to push out of the way with its backhoe. And then even bigger ones that stop traffic in both directions for days. One year, there were thirteen slides between here and New Arenal in a single storm.

Small springs in summer swell to raging torrents in October that take out bridges, sweep away houses, and drown livestock in the lowlands. Even here in the highlands, the damage can be dramatic. The *quebrada* on the west side of the house roars with its extra load of water. Once, the bridge in front of the old coffee-processing plant washed out, so there was no vehicle traffic between Tilarán and New Arenal for three weeks, when the government finally threw up a Bailey bridge. A year later, the route to Quebrada Grande was cut off. Once, we had non-stop heavy rain for thirteen hours. In that storm an ancient *cedro* tree gave way on the far bank of the *quebrada* and, falling with the might of thunder, took out five trees on our side in seconds.

It's cold, clammy, a time for multiple layers of clothing, socks, extra blankets. Roger and I hole up in the bedroom in the evenings with all the doors and windows shut and the fireplace crackling. We feel safe and toasty, the sound of rain lashing against the roof of our shelter. We eat dinner on TV tables and read or watch a movie before crawling under the covers. There's comfort in knowing we have a snug haven in the storm. The weather is impressive, but we've got it licked and feel smug.

Until the electricity goes off.

Complaining bitterly about the damage the rain is doing to his garden, Evelio is fantasizing about his next cash crop (he hasn't had one yet), and he's been to the Ministry of Agriculture (MAG) to see what kind of support they can offer the small agriculturalist of scarce resources. With the international food crisis and the doubling of prices on basic grains here in Costa Rica, the government is offering help to small growers, so now Evelio wants to plant *frijoles,* black beans – something assured of a market, because (he points out) Costa Ricans, *ticos,* eat beans for breakfast, lunch, and dinner. It remains to be seen if he will continue to grow other vegetables, or to stage his plantings so that we can enjoy cucumbers for more than a week.

Finally a day of sun, and you can almost *hear* the photosynthesis in my pots of herbs on the verandah. Basil, mint, rosemary, Chinese oregano, parsley, sage, and chives – these are the staples lined up against the south rail where they are now getting direct afternoon sun. It's the first day that we are noticeably past the autumn equinox. Here in the tropics the sun is almost directly overhead, the length of days varying by no more than an hour from the summer to the winter solstice. We've become attuned to this subtlety, noting that the sun shines on the south side of the house in winter, on the north side in summer. So wonderfully obvious near the equator, this grand tilting of the planet!

Walking in the yard this afternoon, I see chewed parts of cucumbers everywhere. Evelio calls Fortuna *La Destructora*, the Destroyer.

The *jocote* is losing its leaves. I was outside this afternoon sitting in one of the Adirondack chairs in the "outdoor room" above the rock garden. There's a perfect little grove there with the heavy *jocote* and the pines on one side and the *madero negro* and *uruca* trees on the other, peaceful and out of the wind. Our pet cemetery is there, and it's a sweet spot for it. Leaning back and looking up at the massive branches of the *jocote* with their weight of bromeliads and other epiphytes, I could sense that the foliage looked thinner – I could see more sky. And then I remembered that it's autumn in the northern hemisphere and the deciduous trees will be losing their leaves. The small stone pathway through the rock garden is littered with them.

There are fewer deciduous trees in the tropics than in the north, but we have some notable examples here – the long rows of *robles* along the driveway, the *corteza amarillo*, and the *guanacaste* tree just behind the house where the *quebrada* turns to head more westerly. When these trees are bare, the quality of light around the house becomes more watery, less saturated. The sky then reminds me of the *northern* sky on a clear, dry day in winter.

There aren't a lot of clues as to what season we're in here in Costa Rica. We joke when we say there are only two seasons, rainy and windy, but in fact our neighbors refer to a sunny day as "summer" and a rainy day as "winter" even if these days are contiguous. It can even be summer in the morning and winter in the afternoon. We've gotten into the habit of thinking this way, too, after so many years in the country. Not infrequently one has to stop and think: what month are we in? The signs that we are moving through fall, for example, are fewer and far more subtle here where it's green all year round. It's good to get into

18

the habit of paying closer attention.

Meanwhile, the garden is growing ... sideways. Evelio's found a few boys from his village to come over here and dig up new earth in an expansion move that will make this agro-plot 65 yards long. (It's already 36 wide.) The boys are earning the right to some of his future *frijoles*. Too bad we're not crazy about *frijoles*.

Finally, near the end of October, the weather is swinging from the south back into the northeast, the direction the Trade Winds come from. It will back-and-forth like this for a few weeks of transition until, in December, the Trades will be fully back to their old tricks. At this time of year we sometimes witness a collision of the two weathers: a solid wall of water bearing down on us from the eastern end of the lake and a black storm cloud swooping in from the south over the Continental Divide. They do a tug of war out there and nobody wins, except the lake takes on a lot more water, while we stay dry.

By the time the winds reach this end of the lake, they can pack enough punch to do significant damage. Trees down. Service lines down. Roofs blown away. Frequently they blow so hard that the wind turbines on the Continental Divide behind us have to shut down. One year, we had three days of *average* 70 mile-per-hour winds – with gusts over 100 – and one of the old erector-set wind towers just crumpled up and twisted down onto its side. There were so many trees and power lines down that week that we were without electricity for three days.

Is our weather getting more severe? Year-to-year it's hard to tell, without my having kept any records. But anyone over 50 in Tilarán will tell you that it has, that the local climate has, in fact, changed. "It didn't use to be as dry or as windy," the older locals say. Why? "There were a lot more trees."

In fact, the weather *is* changing. We have it officially from the Meteorological Service that the dry season is coming early this year, and we'll be in the "transition" for three-to-five weeks before the rain stops. Here on the lake, however, it doesn't feel like a transition; it feels like a Big Wind socking us in the jaw with a cold front from the north. The rain is driving in under the roof of the verandah at a 45-degree angle and the temperature has dropped into the sixties. This morning I did yoga on the leeward side of the verandah and I wore long sleeves and a hat!

I don't remember ever seeing the cold fronts come through this early. In fact, I distinctly remember a conversation on a December evening in 1990 on a balcony overlooking the Grecia Park. Our tico hosts described the change of season as a cold wind that suddenly arrived out of the north *on December 15th,* which traditionally started people thinking about Christmas.

It takes a while to get used to the wind. At first, it seems to be drumming on the inside of your head. The whole house thrums, the skylight rattles, doors bang, windows whistle, the chimneys sing. Walking around the corner of the verandah, you have to bend forward so as not to have the breath knocked out of you. There are times when I wish the wind would go away – mostly when I'm huddled up in multiple layers of clothing and sticking my fingers under my arms to keep them warm. It's the cold that comes with the wind that gets me. The sound is just Nature howling out her pain through the planet's long winter night. I can live with that.

Walking back from the road with the newspaper the other day, I counted three strangler fig seedlings in an advanced stage of development. The first time I saw one of these, just an odd leaf growing out of the bark of a *uruca* tree, I asked Koki what it was. *Higuerón,* he said. I was amazed at my luck finding a baby fig tree (not aware it was a strangler) to pry away and stick into a bonsai pot, which I did. Free tree, I thought. Now I know better.

The strangler will kill its host tree, sending roots down to the ground and eventually enveloping the other in a slow squeeze, like a boa constrictor. The locals call this *matapalo,* tree-killer. As the old tree dies, it rots away, leaving a hollow in the middle of the new growth, much utilized as shelter by birds and small forest mammals. The new figs I saw the other day started out as just the odd leaf or two. All three now have one strong, thick root firmly attached to the earth, each almost two yards long, and the odd leaf or two are now branching vigorously. "How have I missed this development?" I asked myself. The thought of a quick tree-rescue flitted through my mind. Of the three victims, I love the pine the most, one of a trio bending over the pet cemetery. But that pine is already leaning precariously across the driveway, battered by the Trade Winds for fifty years or more. It'll fall one of these years. Maybe the strangler fig will help to prop it up a while longer. The fact is that the figs themselves turn into huge, magnificent trees, so I shouldn't mind having more around us. I will enjoy watching how they develop from scratch.

I remember the sound and smell of a northern October

wind, a sneaky gust of air bearing the chill scent of winter-to-come, skittering dry leaves across the road, swirling around my legs and rattling my paper bag, as I plodded along on Halloween nights to the clutch of houses a mile down the road. I had an inkling of that same wind last night.

Was my little sister Alison in tow on those Halloween nights? Surely, although I wouldn't have taken her hand. It says a lot about the time and place – 1958, rural Pennsylvania – that our parents allowed two little girls to walk a mile and back on a dark, deserted country road for Halloween treats. We had no fear. But our parents weren't paying much attention to us anyway, because they were in a crisis – the biggest one yet – which was to bring major changes for all of us for decades to come.

Meals were taken in heavy quiet at the kitchen table, the family silenced by our father's tight-lipped rage. Being the elder sister, I assumed that he was angry at *me*. That was the year I started eating compulsively. I would come in from school and make myself *four* pieces of cinnamon toast, heaped with sugar and dripping with butter. It didn't help that in the late afternoons I would find Mom leaning against the back of the sofa, reading, feet propped on the coffee table, with a beer-mug full of gin and tonic at her side. The first thing I had to do, while she went into the kitchen to start dinner, was practice the piano. I wasn't allowed to do that after Dad got home.

In my first major act of shooting myself in the foot, I announced one evening that I was quitting piano lessons. Four years were enough, I said. Too much. My parents turned their mutual wrath on me, and I was cowed into going on. (Even though it was guilt that kept me at it, I'm glad they forced me to continue, and I studied long enough to give myself years of pleasure afterwards.)

It was around that same time that I injured my back. I had spent my twelfth summer learning how to dive from the one-meter and three-meter boards at the country club swimming pool. I had a crush on the instructor and probably went off those boards fifty times a day. I loved the sense of free fight over the blue water, of turning my awkward pre-teen body into a winged bird. That winter our youth fellowship group went for an evening swim at the high school, and, without testing the tension of the board, I decided to show off with a high jackknife that landed me in the water at a bad angle and herniated a disc. I could barely pull myself out of the pool to lie flat on the coping. In those days nobody knew about herniated discs or what to do about them, so I suffered intermittent and sometimes severe lumbar pain until a surgery when I was 40. I have often wondered at the timing of that injury; it brought me a lot of attention from my father, who had always been so difficult to please. And what was my sister doing while I was soaring? Swimming underwater, from one end of the pool to the other. It was her own way of hiding, as our mother sat drinking at the 19th hole.

We didn't learn until we were in our twenties what the nature of that distant marital crisis was – our mother's infidelity unmasked – although throughout our teens, my sister and I each harbored our unspoken suspicions. It is a judgmental age; so easy to blame, so difficult to see into the hurting heart of another, especially a parent. Alison and I carried this sense of betrayal – and in my case, the fear that I was doomed to be like our mother – into later life, when, in our separate ways, we could finally see that her love for us was greater than our grief.

October wind. These hints of northern weather I'm sensing around me – light, sound, smell – are tantalizing here in my tropical home. I need to translate those old sensations into my current reality; opening up to my environment is an exercise in countless associations that, albeit painful, enrich the here and now.

The Lake

The sign that stood in front of the new gas station announced 704 meters of altitude (2300 feet). It marked the Continental Divide, the highest point on the road between Cinco Esquinas (Five Corners) and the town of Tilarán to the south. Cinco Esquinas is the most important landmark for vehicular traffic on Lake Arenal, dividing the road into the two branches that take you along either its southern or its northern shore. Until recently, there were no signs telling you which was which.

From Cinco Esquinas, the right-hand, or southern, road dips sharply down into the village of San Luis, revealing the broadening expanse of the lake as it descends, until finally the road rounds a curve and the whole length and breadth of the water shimmers at the foot of *Volcán Arenal*.

Sometimes the wind rips the surface of the lake, pushing big, white-capped waves all the way from the volcano to the western shore. At other times the water is as still as a mirror, deep and green and cold, reflecting the surrounding emerald hills with their pied cattle and dark patches of forest along the tumbling rivers. The volcano is an almost perfect cone, a foreign object set thoughtlessly down among the old round hills, its strange bulk looming at the eastern end of the lake, belching smoke and rocks and roaring like a chained spirit.

Rainbows are common around Lake Arenal, where the sun frequently shines in one place even while it's raining in another. Sometimes, because of the sharply curving road, it almost seems as if you can pass under a rainbow.

From San Luis, the paved road along the south shore of the lake extends to just inside the far boundary of New

Tronadora, where the asphalt abruptly stops and the road continues in a series of partially graveled ruts and potholes until it degenerates to a bare cow track, traversing several rickety bridges and passing Old Tronadora before it finally arrives at the bank of the Río Chiquito, too deep to cross except in dry season.

In Old Tronadora, one of the towns that were mostly flooded when the dam was built at the eastern end of the lake, several horses are parked in front of the original *cantina*, patiently awaiting the whim of their owners. The farther the road wends along the south shore, the lonelier it becomes, until on the near bank of the Río Chiquito civilization seems to have disappeared. Upriver, there's a remote village and an abandoned gold mine, but here the only looming presence is the volcano. If there were a bridge – even a few rough planks – you could circumnavigate the lake. But you walk out into the middle of the stony, clear-flowing river and know it would be foolish to try the car in the thigh-high water. On one of our excursions along the beautiful south shore, a small boy in an ageless floppy hat approached the opposite bank on the bare back of his mare. Gingerly, the horse picked her way across the swift current, and we suddenly realized we were using the wrong transport for the place and time.

The left fork at Cinco Esquinas leads around the western edge of the lake past our house to the north shore and New Arenal, where the old road used to rattle your teeth for five killing miles until it smoothed out again to lead you to the dam and the other world that is the *cantón* of San Carlos, where it rains twice as much as where we are. The farther east you go, the lusher and junglier the vegetation; at the foot of the volcano bright impatiens nod alongside the road, ropey lianas dangle threateningly overhead and leaves the size of elephant ears encroach on the right-of-way. The road these days is paved except for a few bumpy stretches and a tiny, under-cut ford that looks threatening even in dry season. But even though the time to get to the eastern end of the lake is shortened, you still feel you've traveled to another country.

From the gas station on the Continental Divide, the road winds sharply south through a series of breakneck curves to the one-lane bridge below the entrance to Tilarán. The old school buses and overburdened cattle trucks gear down for the bridge and then roar through their changes up into town. The buses all have brightly painted names on their sides – Invincible, Galileo, Pacific Princess, Brawling Woman, and the mysterious Istanbul Express. Farm workers, crowded into the backs of pickup trucks, chatter good-humoredly as their vehicles list around the curves.

At end of day, ragged clumps of white fog tear themselves away from the valley of the Río Santa Elena, that runs past Tilarán, and drift lazily up the mountainsides to join the panoply of the sunset sky. The fog brings an eerie silence in which the distant sounds near and the near sounds far – the roaring of the howler monkeys along the riverbed, the lonely *wheep-wheep* of a night bird, the *clop-clop* of a horse and rider late returning home. Each thing sounds isolated and clear, its direction masked by the tricky fog.

As night falls, the traffic stops, the silence draws in, and giant moths bounce against the long fluorescent lights at the gas station. For a while after the station opened, the man on the night shift collected these moths in a net and mounted them with pins on thin sheets of Styrofoam to sell to the tourists. But that man is gone now, just as the altitude sign is now gone. He's been replaced by a sleepy-eyed boy propped on a small wooden stool leaning against the garage wall.

When the fog lifts, the lights of Tilarán twinkle, secure in the deep bowl of the valley. Some nights the moon limns the purple shadows of the surrounding mountains, and the elusive Southern Cross seems tipped on the spire of the church, but most nights the town just gleams, suspended in empty space. At dawn Tilarán's lights go out and its buildings glow red and white in the fresh light, the bulky white steeple of the church catching the first rays of morning.

There's a wind tunnel on the Continental Divide a little before the gas station, where all the trees lean in the same direction, as if they wanted to go somewhere. Decades and decades of the winter Trade Winds have given them a yearning look, limbs all reaching to the southwest overlooking the long, wide Guanacaste Plain and the western ridges of the *Sierra de Nicoya*, the boundary of the endless Pacific. It's hot in the lowlands, but here, at 704 meters of altitude, it's cool, even just ten degrees north of the equator.

This is where I live and write: with my new husband and an assortment of pets in our new "tropical" house, the Tilarán Mountains to the southeast, the backbone of the Americas (the *Cordillera Central*) to the northwest, anchored by an active volcano on one of the most beautiful lakes in the world.

November
Living on the Land

Evelio's patience is wearing thinner. Twice now I've tried to talk to him about patience, even telling him that gringos are well-known for their *im*patience, that I've had to learn mine from *his* culture, and that he is in no way setting an example for me. He smiles at this, but the economic facts are such that he feels he needs to make money with this agricultural project and, as long as it's organic, the financial return is looking too small for the amount of work he's putting into it. The Ministry of Agriculture has evaluated his case and decided he's not poor enough to merit a subsidy. They have assured him that his returns will rise with each year as the soil improves, so he needs to wait it out.

Yesterday we had our closest thing yet to an argument:

"I want to use a little fertilizer to jump-start the *frijoles*" he had the nerve to tell me.

I went from zero to impatient in a nanosecond. "What? What kind of fertilizer?"

"Just a teeny bit" – he started backing up – "whatever I can buy at Jenkins's store."

I supposed he was looking for a little money to pay for this, otherwise he probably wouldn't have mentioned it, but I know Jenkins doesn't sell anything remotely organic. Old Harry Jenkins sits by the window of his dusty wooden feed store like Jabba the Hutt, baiting every environmentalist that walks in the door, including me.

"You know that will contaminate the soil, Evelio. And not only will it contaminate the soil *now*, it will mean that nothing you plant in there will be certifiably organic for three years." He decided he didn't believe me, and I had to remind him, my voice rising, that we had an agreement that he could till this plot only if it were organic. He nodded and hopped the bus back to MAG to talk to the government agronomist.

Later, he told me the agronomist confirmed what I had said, and he seemed resigned to continuing the experiment (with periodic infusions of cash from us).

I can see how he is getting discouraged. He brought me a couple of ears of the Hawaiian sweet corn, half rotted from the heavy rains and picked over by birds and bugs. *All* the corn had been beaten up by the untimely wind, but the Hawaiian we'd had special hopes for. Our dreams of eating sweet corn on the cob will have to be postponed, and we agree Evelio will try to salvage what he can for seed for next year. Now we have a scarecrow in the garden, a simple bamboo cross draped with a large black plastic garbage bag and a smaller white bag for its head. It flaps in the breeze and makes the dogs bark.

More than once I've had a Costa Rican "nostalgia conversation," but I still remember the first with José Adémar many years ago. Like a lot of people around here, he grew up in the remote countryside where people had lived for generations a simple, rural, self-sufficient lifestyle. They grew their own corn, beans and vegetables. Their livestock provided meat and milk. They made their own cheese, raised cane for sugar, ground corn, kept chickens for eggs, even grew and roasted their coffee. The only transportation was of the four-legged variety: horse, mule, oxen or all three. Family tended to stay in one place, so that sooner or later everybody in an area was related in one way or another. José Adémar was hankering after the simplicity of those days, and I think he was feeling a little remorseful at the increasing middle-class complexities of his life.

The other day Evelio was singing the same tune. His father and one of his brothers *still* live that way on a piece of land uphill from Sabalito – although they have electricity and a pickup truck. Our housekeeper Rosa's parents just recently moved off their land to a small house in Río Piedras. They never had electricity or a truck, and her father never missed a day's work in his 79 years. Now, in his new house, he's had to buy a fridge, an electric stove (Rosa's mother cooked over a wood fire), a TV, and a rice cooker. Once all that was in place, he went to the hospital with stomach cancer.

Evelio and I were standing on the front steps looking out over the garden as he spoke about the kind of independence living on the land brings, and I could see he yearned to have it for himself.

"Do you know that most of the vegetables we eat have to come four hours up the *Interamericana* from San José?" he asked me.

I hadn't known that.

"But what about the ones grown here?" I asked.

"It's an *ironía*" – irony – "they get bought up by a wholesaler who takes them to San José for auction, where they are bought by the supermarket chains who then distribute them right back where they came from."

I found this disheartening. "But what about the Central Market in Tilarán? Surely that's local produce."

He shook his head.

I thought about an article I'd read once about the "hundred-mile diet," in which people make a concerted effort to eat only things produced within a hundred-mile radius, thus reducing the petro-load on their food. Evelio liked that idea.

Many of us look back on simpler pre-war times with the same kind of nostalgia Adémar and Evelio express. The difference in Costa Rica is that this rural memory is more recent. Evelio is almost young enough to be my son; his father is still living off the land. Costa Rica's entrance into the developing world covers only a single generation. Perhaps because these changes are happening so quickly, the memory, the hankering after the traditional lifestyle, is more powerful. More important, the skills and the knowledge necessary to survive on the land are still intact. And perhaps for this reason, the necessary adjustments to the rigors of climate change won't be so drastic here as elsewhere. I hope not.

November rolled in on a white fog. The wind died and it felt as if we were riding a boat in a dense white sea, all sounds around us muffled except for the sharp, rippling call of an *oropéndola* in the eucalyptus next to the house. Living on the second floor of the building as we do, with open wooden decks all around, exaggerates this feeling of isolation, as if the tricky old fog were swirling around underneath us, too. The roar of the creek has damped down to a dull murmur, a car on the road to a soft *whoosh*. Water condenses on the window screens, enclosing us even further. We chase away the chill with a blaze in the fireplace.

On a clear day, the view fills you up. When the view shuts down, as now, it feels as if our souls have shrunk.

Last night we were awakened by the dogs barking at the cry of an animal in the *quebrada*. At first I thought it was a bird, but the sound was too big, too intermittent and desperate. Then, over the accompaniment of the dogs, the cry grew even more urgent and breathy, its pitch dropping bit by bit until, finally, it was choked off. The dogs quieted immediately. We suspect a boa got hold of something. Midnight drama in the jungle.

Even though the rains have diminished, the lake continues to rise. There's still plenty of rain in the pre-montane cloud forests of the uplands; since everything in this watershed flows into the lake, all the extra groundwater is finding its way there, too. Lake-level watching is a favorite local pastime, since we all know that a full lake at the end of rainy season means a longer part of the dry season without serious electrical outages. Even though Lake Arenal is one of the most beautiful I've ever seen, we never forget its real function—hydroelectric power. Today the lake a mirror, not a breath of wind stirring the reflection of the black-green hills and empty white sky. The deep, silvered water itself seems to be waiting for something to happen.

Adémar and I have been friends ever since he built the vacation home for my parents on the small lot next door to my ex-husband and me. This was supposed to be a guest house so that they could be more comfortable when they visited, but when my mother got hold of the idea she turned it into a full-sized home. I think she had a secret wish to stay in Costa Rica. Since my parents were absent half the time, I became the construction supervisor - it was the first time I had ever built a house - and I learned a lot from

Adémar. It was a good experience also because it kept me out of my own house and away from my husband, who was drinking too heavily to get involved. And it was good to stretch my skills and feel competent again. But it was a complicated year because I was also having an affair.

This was a calculated decision, and I chose someone who had no importance for me beyond his physical attraction. My husband had long been blaming me for our lousy sex life, calling me frigid and worse. The last time I had come home from San José to find him passed out on the living room rug, something swept through me with the power of a revelation, and I knew that I neither loved him nor would I try anymore. I was going to live my own life. While the affair lasted only a short time, it proved that everything was still in perfect working order, and it emboldened me.

At some point during that year, I decided I was going to leave the marriage, and, even before I told my husband, I confessed what I was thinking to my father. It was obvious he found this most inconvenient since he and my mother were planning on spending three months out of every six living next door. He wasn't at all sympathetic – just plain annoyed. And he said something I will never forget: "Why don't you just stay married and be miserable like the rest of us?"

In that last year we were together, my husband brought Roger home for dinner. He did this occasionally, invited total strangers home, almost always unattached gringos who hung out at Mary's Bar and Hotel in the mornings for coffee or a stiff pick-me-up.

I didn't warm to Roger particularly. Frankly, I was inclined to be a little suspicious of people my husband liked. But we passed a pleasant enough evening.

Months later, riding my mare up past the all-night gas station, I rounded a curve and saw a small house in a messy state of renovation. Something compelled me to pull into the gate and dismount. Inside, Roger was working up a sweat with a handsaw over lengths of tongue-and-groove *cedro* for the facing of a breakfast bar. I asked if I could look around, and as I explored the small rooms with their oversized windows and stepped back out onto the front porch, a giddy joy filled me up. The view over the Guanacaste Plain was long. I could live here, I thought ... and a plan for leaving my marriage came into focus.

I moved in when the house was still unfinished, and Roger showed up once in a while to smooth out the details. Although we chatted amicably enough, I kept to myself. Living alone after 16 years in a bad marriage was simple glory. I was writing day and night, practicing the piano, dancing to old Ray Charles cassettes, serving up my dinners to candle-light. I had no car or phone, but friends would drop in. To supplement the small share my husband had agreed to, I gave swimming lessons, piano lessons. I bussed or hitched into town and felt happy as a bird on a wire.

Several months later, my landlady invited me to a noisy party over in New Arenal. Roger was there, and we danced. We danced a lot, and something finally sparked. It turned out to be powerful enough that eventually we decided we could share our poverty together. He moved into the "house on the hill on the curve," as the locals called it, and our relationship deepened over the course of some very happy – and some very difficult – times.

Now that half of the foliage has fallen from the *jocote*

tree, it's easier to see all the *other* things that are growing on it – mosses, crinkly gray-green lichens, baby air plants, delicate vines and five-gallon bromeliads – a whole ecosystem supported by this one tree. And an ecosystem with*in* an ecosystem is a bromeliad, home to dozens of creatures, insects, and amphibians, who depend on the pool of water always at its heart. Bromeliads in nurseries are surely bred to retain their flowers, and there are dozens of showy varieties. But in the wild, the blooming isn't usually so dramatic or long-lived.

Today, sitting in the Adirondack chair after my walk down to the gate, I see one of the five bromeliads on the *jocote* starting to flower. The stalk rising from the center of the plant must be a yard high, with seven branches, each bearing up to eighteen green and purple pods. I'll keep an eye on this one so I can catch it at full bloom. There's another one blooming in the pineapple patch. Pineapples are bromeliads too, but they take as many as eighteen months to produce a ripe fruit. Right now, all we have is the mauve, tightly packed flower beginning to rise from the center of the oldest plant.

When we eat a pineapple, we plant the spiky top right back in the pineapple patch. Since there are never more than six or seven plants in the patch, it's a long time between pineapples around here. I could buy them at the store, but it's more fun to eat the ones we tend at home.

Next year I'll watch more closely, because I don't want to miss as many tangerines as we've missed this year. We have a couple of *mandarino* trees, and they're off my regular walking route. By the time I came across them this year, the fruit was already two-thirds gone and there were dozens half-eaten by the birds on the ground. There were also tangerine skins scattered about, indicating some two-legged frugivore. I asked Koki to be sure and tell me when the *mandarinas* come in next time, because we like to eat them, too. "I didn't know you liked them," he said. After all these years of working for us, he didn't know we liked them? And when we're buying navel oranges at the supermarket for a dollar a piece? I made him go harvest a basketful, which he had to scale the trees to do since all the easy pickings were long gone.

When Roger and I moved into the little house on this property in 1998, there were already lots of different fruit trees around: papayas, sweet lemons, *criollo* lemons (like key limes), avocados, oranges and bananas of every stripe, guavas, and even a grapefruit tree. With all these riches, we quickly grew lazy. Pruning, fertilizing, and picking is work, and finally we were happy to let others do the picking and carry away most of the fruit for free. In the early years, I tried to keep up with the pruning, at least of the young trees we planted ourselves, but citrus wood is *hard,* and my arthritic hands soon gave up. Untended, these trees have since gone wild. There's intentional organic farming, and organic by inattention. The latter is all we had around here until Evelio started his garden.

The other day, Evelio was preparing the front door for a new coat of varnish, when he noticed some little green balls on the decking around one of the potted *ficus* trees. He called me out to look at them. They looked as if they had been chewed, but Evelio informed me that they were *caca,* caterpillar droppings. We both looked up at the *ficus* tree and observed that a number of the upper branches were bare. We peered into the remaining foliage for some minutes before Evelio spotted it: about six inches long, gray and brown, with I-don't-know-how-many little black feet clinging to the branch, steadily chewing its way through every leaf in sight. It was beautifully camouflaged to look exactly like a *ficus* branch. I said the Spanish equivalent of "yuck," (¡Qué asco!) and begged Evelio to kill it. It was a little tricky for him to get hold of – wiggly – but finally he was able to cart it away.

I know that caterpillars turn into beautiful giant moths and brightly colored butterflies, but I will brook no competition for the life of my ornamental plants. As Costa Rican ornamentals go, these *ficus* were not cheap. Somebody had painstakingly woven five small *ficus* trees together to form what are essentially large bonsai and maintained them until the trunks melded together in a hollowed-out braided form that is very decorative. I have them planted in large Mexican pots on either side of the front door, where they have been through a lot – buffeted by wind, attacked by aphids, scale, and other infestations – and I will kill to keep them alive.

There are some smaller *ficus* bonsai downstairs, and I went looking for any similar damage. Sure enough, I found another of the awful creatures. To get rid of it without having to squish it, I sprayed it with Malathion (which sadly did *not* immediately kill the poor thing), and I repotted the plant, carrying the pot-full of old dirt and half-dead caterpillar out to the trash, where I knew it would sooner or later be cremated. This did not make me feel like a good environmentalist.

It's a delicate subject: gardening organic while the bugs are eating your crops. The most prolific are the *zompopas*, leaf-cutter ants. They seem to pop up out of nowhere and will denude a good-sized shrub in a night, traveling to and from their nest in such numbers that they trample the grass down to bare dirt. It's these very obvious two-lane highways that Koki follows to track down their nest and pump it full of insecticide. Leafcutters are highly coordinated social creatures. They don't eat the leaves but use them to feed a complex mold that they cultivate for their larvae in a special chamber deep in their nests. Incredible little farmers, these. I have read that leafcutters move more earth than any other creature on the planet, millions and millions of tons a year. If something threatens the mold, they will carve off the contaminated portion and remove it, digging new tunnels to carry it away. A nest can have hundreds of entrances and exits. Pumping lethal chemicals into it is not going to kill it off, just slow the ants down and keep them busy for a while doing something other than eating your ornamentals. Sooner or later, the nest will pop up in another location and begin its damage anew. It's war.

And this is why I waited with such interest to see what Evelio would do when the *zompopas* discovered his vegetable garden. He bought a simple pump, just a hollow cylinder with a pumping handle on top and a flexible hose coming out near the bottom. The powdered insecticide goes into a little cup at the bottom of the cylinder. One day I observed him crawling through the barbed-wire fence into our neighbor's overgrown pasture – from where the army of *zompopas* was obviously marching – carrying his new pump. There's no way there's anything organic about the contents of that pump. But at least so far, the leafcutters have not built a nest within the boundaries of the garden. And, because of the slope of the land, rain runoff will carry the poison away from his crops, and some day through the ground water and into the lake. (Sadly, this is happening all around the lake, and the use of agrichemicals is a big environmental issue here as elsewhere. All we can do is try to use as little as we can until there are safe biological alternatives.)

I finally bought the Spanish edition of Ed Bernhardt's *The Costa Rican Organic Home Gardening Guide,* which Evelio has been reading avidly, especially the part about natural remedies to control insects. Yesterday at dusk, he bicycled over here in a lather, carrying a handful of little plastic plates and asking for a beer to put out for the slugs. I wonder if the leafcutters like beer, too.

We read recently about the increasing population of two kinds of poisonous snakes in a reserve near the northern Meseta Central town of San Ramón. The reserve is a cloud forest, like the much more famous Monteverde just south of here. University of Costa Rica herpetology students have been monitoring the snake population for several years. When they see one, they catch it, note its weight and other data, and then mark it so it can be identified in the future. They attribute the increasing population of these two species to less rainfall in the reserve, a direct result of climate change. Drier weather is favorable to the survival of snake offspring. They also suggest the possibility of a newly created imbalance between the snakes and their few predators. A chilling thought.

My father liked snakes and, when I was a little girl, he used to catch them, feed them and let them go. I remember my horrified fascination watching a snake consume a toad in the bottom of an old wastebasket. There are family legends about Dad and his pet snake collection when he was a boy. He had a naturalist's lively curiosity about *all* living things. But, even as he tried to teach me not to fear snakes, and even though I have handled a few harmless ones in my day, and even though I've read enough to know that I have several hours to get to help if I'm ever bitten by a fer-de-lance or a coral snake, I have a proper horror of snakes, period. My sister does, too, and she has a hard time understanding why I would live in a country with 17 species of poisonous snakes.

If I had to face all these snakes on a daily basis, I wouldn't live here either. But in all my years in Costa Rica, I have seen only three coral snakes, one eyelash viper and one pelagic sea snake, the only poisonous species in the Eastern Pacific. None of them seemed interested in attacking me at the time. I have a healthy respect for them, though, and have learned to watch where I'm walking and, if I'm in the woods, keep my peripheral vision lively because many snakes are arboreal. As with most other creatures in the wild, they won't bother you if you don't bother them. Most of the snake-bite victims in this country are farm workers who accidentally step on a snake. And 99 percent of them live to tell the tale.

How many times I have rescued a hummingbird! And each is a moment of magic. The very first was in our first year in the country near Grecia, when at nightfall a hummingbird became confused between the glass and the security bars outside the kitchen window. I somehow knew I could capture the thing in my hands if I were just patient enough. Outside, I slowly brought my cupped hands closer and closer to the bird until – oh, what a precious fragile thing! – I held it loosely in my hands, feeling its tiny heart thudding against my fingers. I turned, took a few steps and tossed up my hands into the dark to free it.

Yesterday, a hummingbird slipped in through an open verandah door. We didn't realize we had a captive until, in a sudden scuffle, one of the cats caught it. Roger lunged for the cat and grabbed her before she squirmed under the bed with her prize. I pried open her jaws and the undamaged bird flew up to the ceiling, beating its little head repeatedly in its panic. While Roger took the cat, I closed the interior doors and grabbed a broom, thinking I could gently swoosh it toward the open verandah door and freedom. But it kept eluding me, until finally, tired out, it slid down a wall and came to a stop on the floor. I approached it slowly (by now I'm an old hand at this!), hands cupped, and caught it. Just a single flicker of wing against my palm, and I released it to the verandah.

I believe the birds know I'm not going to harm them. I have rescued plenty of them from the cats, and sometimes a bird will stun itself against a window. I pick it up or pry it loose and, if it's unconscious, I park it in one of the hanging ferns to recover where the cats can't get it. But if conscious, once they're in my hands, they stop fluttering and struggling and stay perfectly still until I can find a safe place to put them.

Although I grew up in the country, I took the natural world mostly for granted. Beyond the obvious things, I never learned the names of trees, flowers or stars. I almost flunked Biology. Birdwatching, I thought, was for sissies. The outdoors for me were a rough-and-tumble, tomboy world, a welcome escape from the dysfunctional "indoors" of my family. I was lucky to have that escape. Perhaps now, in my third age, I am escaping into it again – escaping from the pains of age and advancing disability – only this time I have found the inner connection to it that wasn't there before. From the natural world now I draw spiritual strength, and that gives me joy.

Last night as we were getting ready for bed, I saw a strange oblong shape moving on the outside of our bedroom window. I sneaked over and put on my glasses for a closer look. I was staring at the underside of a praying mantis-type insect, three inches long, pale green, and with two wide flat carapaces, one over the thorax, the other over the head. From underneath it looked as if it were wearing a coolie hat. There were plenty of other insects on the glass, many of them pale parchment-colored moths, and others almost too small to see in the light from our bedside lamp. The mantis's movements reminded me of the motion of single-celled creatures under a microscope, jostling each other like the bumper cars at the fair. With its right foreleg, it guided itself around while with its left it scooped little insects into its mouth. It was getting a bug about every two seconds. I called Roger over, and we both watched for several minutes, entranced. Beats television.

A land bridge between two continents, Costa Rica has more wildlife than most other places on the planet, including an estimated 35,000 forms of bug life. (This is not a place for the squeamish). I have books on mammals, amphibians, plants, trees, and snakes, but if anyone has catalogued all the insects in this country, I haven't yet seen the book in print. It would have to be a work in progress. It is estimated that up to 25 percent of the biodiversity in Costa Rica has yet to be discovered.

Yesterday we woke to a white fog, and all-day squalls blew through on the Trade Winds, flattening Evelio's last standing corn. Today, the anemometer at Cinco Esquinas is registering sustained winds of 40 knots that are driving a horizontal rain. I saw Evelio walk out to the garden today during a lull, shoulders hunched in defeat. Now he's talking about growing organic crops under cover, and he has a new fantasy about a bamboo structure covered with plastic.

I reminded him once again that the only way to achieve controlled conditions is with irrigation, which costs *us* money (electricity to run the well and pressure pumps), but now he has a scheme to capture rainwater from the plastic roof of his non-existent shelter with a tank and drip system. He'll need PVC rain gutters, pipe, a tank with a lid so the mosquitoes don't breed in it, a structure to keep the tank in the air to achieve a gravity flow, and perforated hose. I wonder how much all *this* is going to cost.

This morning Evelio arrived in a *taxi carga* with four or five lengths of cheap lumber. I hallooed him from the verandah and asked him what it was for.

"I'm building another worm box," he said. He was referring to the casket-like structure where his California red worms are ever-more-rapidly chewing their way through our neighbor's horse manure. I asked him why he needed another worm box, and he said that the worms are reproducing at such a rate that they need more room.

My next question was tinged with anxiety: "And where are you going to put the new box?" I was thinking about the small woodshed that he's converted to Organic Gardening Central, where the worm casket on its sawhorses takes up almost all the available dirt floor space.

"I'm going to put it under the current one," he answered.

"Ah, *bueno*," said I. "And what happens when the worms outgrow the new box?"

"I'll build another and put it between the top one and the bottom one."

I was having trouble controlling my distress at visions of worm caskets sprouting up all over the property.

"*What* are you going to do with these millions of

worms?"

"I'm making fertilizer," he said.

"I *know* you're making fertilizer, but do you intend to commercialize it? Are you going to sell or give away some of the worms? What happens when they outgrow the *third* box?" I just wasn't getting through.

"We could put them in the garden," he suggested.

I began to see these worms as tipping the balance of the ecosystem of our farm; I imagined the soil all around us literally aboil with California red worms.

"Evelio, are you sure it's all right to release them, where they might interfere with other creatures in the environment?"

His face screwed into a puzzle for a moment, and then he got it, and he said he'd consult with the expert on vermiculture at the National Learning Institute.

In a photocopied book he'd picked up at a seminar on greenhouse gardening, I read that, under ideal conditions, California red worms live up to 15 years. They'll eat almost all kitchen scraps (except citrus rinds), but their favorite food of all is horse manure, which they turn into compost at a truly alarming rate. I suppose we could slow them down by giving them food they don't like. And I imagine that, in the not-too-distant future, our neighbor's horses will not be able to keep up with the demand. I'll have to tell my friend Alejo how well the initial half-kilo of worms he gave us is prospering so he can let other interested parties know. It would be a relief to be able to share all this wealth.

December
Bad Fences Make Bad Neighbors

There was a respite of only two days before the weather closed down again, and we've been living through wave after wave of cold fronts rolling in from the north. Without central heating, the house feels damp, our toes never quite dry out in our socks, the flagstones in the atrium are icy, and everything smells of wet cat. When it's like this, the cats get cabin fever and several times a day chase each other around the house in a frenzy, bouncing from table to chair to rug to piano to table, and I fear for the lamps. Bounding into the open piano, they have broken three more of the ancient bass strings, so corroded now that they're almost too delicate to touch.

The other day, driving along a curve in the road, I came across eight black vultures sitting on a row of fence posts, all facing into the wind with their wings fully extended, obviously trying to dry out.

Incredibly in this weather, the volcano was visible briefly one evening at dusk, just the ghost of its shape on the southeastern horizon with its cloud of smoke and ash towering high above. As I watched, a perfectly elliptical flash of faint red light appeared above the cone for no more than a second, the reflection of an explosion in the crater. A minute or two later it happened again, and I went to tell Roger, but by the time he came out to the verandah, the clouds had closed in again.

After another hour-long pep talk yesterday, I agreed to walk the property with Evelio this morning to see if there was a likely spot to plant *frijol tapado* (covered beans). He has been so depressed, as if he personally were being attacked by the weather, and I wanted to give him something else to think about. There's always been two-yard-high scrub on the far side of the fence, the remains of an old orchard. This scrub serves as a windbreak for the first two or three yards of Evelio's plot; everywhere else, the wind has its way. Even some of the low-growing cilantro is being yanked out of the ground by the wind. Now Koki tells Evelio that the guy who is leasing the next-door property for his cows plans to chop everything flat, thus removing our windbreak. We need to look for alternatives.

We walked the fence-line, searching for a place where he could plant. *Frijol tapado* is an ancient method of scattering seeds in an area sufficiently overgrown with scrub that the grass can't grow. Parting the tangle of vines and low shrubs with his hands, he showed me the perfectly clean, black soil underneath. There the bean plants can grow protected from the elements. This is organic gardening at its most primitive, and Evelio was enthusiastic to give it a try. This is also the process by which Nature reforests herself. Under the scrub, seeds dropped by bats, birds, and other animals take root and eventually push themselves above the covering greenery into the light. Evelio showed me half a dozen seedlings within just a yard of where we stood. And he told me their names, too.

We walked a few yards farther to stand under the long limbs of a low-branching fig tree. There we caught glimpses of four or five species of birds feeding on the tiny, reddish fruits covering the branches. There were hundreds of the little figs on the ground – an obvious fig nursery in progress. I fell into the magic of discovery. I never realized before just how knowledgeable Evelio is. Excitedly, I dragged him down to the little runoff creek where there stands a magnificent "combination tree," which Evelio called *primario* – meaning part of what was once primary forest around here. This huge tree is actually at least three different species whose trunks have grown together, and one of them is a strangler fig. Evelio said you can tell it's a strangler by the way it has wrapped itself around the other trunks. The branches of this tree have totally different foliage, one of which in the spring produces sweetly scented white flowers. In addition to vines, bromeliads, air plants, lichens, mosses, and who knows what else this tree is supporting, there is what I call an upside-down plant. It's an epiphyte; you can trace its single root up to where it wraps itself around a heavy branch. Near head-level, the plant branches into hundreds of delicate, pale green tendrils like a chandelier. Evelio said he thinks it's a kind of orchid.

As we walked back toward the house, he showed me some deer tracks. The deer like the scrubby areas because they can be hidden while they forage. In all our years here, I have seen deer only twice. The dogs keep them out of sight, but it's nice to know they're still around. Closer to the house, I pointed out the new strangler fig that has popped up in the pine tree. Evelio showed me how the main root is already developing side shoots that will eventually envelop the tree. He called it the "struggle for survival." I told him I had decided not to try to save the pine, and he agreed. "It's natural," he said.

The reason I had insisted on looking the property over with him before he takes up any more of it for agricultural use is that I didn't want him planting anything on land we would be dedicating to reforestation. But there's a spot at the top of the rise that Roger and I would like to save for a future guest house, and it was here I thought Evelio might find a place to grow his *frijol tapado*. But no, the area was too clean; there wasn't the type of brush that he would need.

"But that's okay," he said. He seemed to be cheering up. "Forests are more important than beans."

Today I drove around to the north shore of the lake to visit Irene. As I turned out of the drive, a pale winter sunlight suffused all I could see. It was the first time I've been able to drive with the windows down in quite a while, and there was a fair breeze rippling the long grasses on the hillsides and blowing through the car, making me feel as if all my senses had awakened after a long sleep. As I passed Equus, a landmark barbecue at the confluence of the Río Sabalo and the lake, I could see just how high the water was – the river mouth had disappeared into a broad water meadow – the lake nearly at its highest. Good news for the electric company, but for some reason it also *feels* good to see the lake so high – with the water this close, the waves seem almost to be lapping at the road in some places. There's an outlet at the volcano end of the lake, which takes the overflow under the dam, so there's no danger of flooding, only erosion, and there are a few places where the water is beginning to undercut the road.

On my way home, I stopped at the nearby windsurf center. I could see Evelio out on a board in his wetsuit, skimming along, his clear plastic sail flashing reflections of the afternoon light.

After the holder of the concession for the windsurf center said he was shutting down for lack of money, Roger and a few others decided they would try to keep it open on a volunteer basis, since this was the only site available during the offseason. They needed someone to stay the night, because there's always a lot of gear out in the open. Evelio agreed. The idea was that Evelio would be the first to be paid out of any earnings. And if there aren't any earnings, Evelio continues to stay there, keeping track of his time so he can be reimbursed later. He lives in an old shipping container. He has electricity (also paid out of the earnings, or out of Roger's pocket if there aren't any earnings) and a cell phone. His television antenna is broken.

Roger has been trying to encourage Evelio to stay at the center during the day if the weather is fair in case people show up wanting to rent equipment or take a lesson. This is so Evelio can make some money. But while he is at the windsurf center, he is not available to do anything I need done around the house. The front door has been sanded and awaiting its varnish for a month now. And he's not spending time in his garden, either. He had someone else out there last week planting beans by the time-honored pole method – poke a stick in the ground, drop in a seed, step on the hole, move six inches and repeat – but the rest of the terrain is looking pretty abandoned. I am trying not to be discouraged about the fact that my to-do list is not being attended to. I am also trying not to feel anxious about Evelio's untended garden.

Down at the windsurf center today the water was high, with a strong surge against the bank. I wandered around a bit, as I watched Evelio get dumped and water-start his rig a couple of times. He looked happy out there. Near the container, there was some laundry flapping on a string tied between two bamboo poles stuck in the ground – a small domestic touch. Along the bank I noticed a few papaya seedlings about a yard high. Evelio's work. And then, in the lee I spied a row of tomato plants, neatly tied up and beginning to droop under the weight of their green fruit. Interspersed among them were some pineapple tops. Of course: Evelio's garden is wherever Evelio happens to be.

Years ago, when we were building this house, Evelio planted tomatoes and papayas behind the construction site. The ground drops off there along the lip of the *quebrada* and so is out of the wind. When I noticed the papayas beginning to fruit, he said the monkeys like them, too. He knows I'm all in favor of planting things that the birds and animals like.

The monkeys don't like just the fruit of the papaya; it's the new leaves that often attract them. I learned this when we moved into the little house, where there used to be three papayas growing between the house and the *quebrada*. A lemon tree provided a handy bridge between the jungle of the *quebrada* and the first two papayas, where the monkeys would routinely strip the new greenery. Monkeys avoid the ground, where they're more vulnerable to predators, and the third papaya tree was just out of reach. I decided to string a stout rope between the second and third papaya trees, then sit on the porch at the side of the house when the monkeys were nearby and wait to see what would happen.

The troop was always led into the papayas by the head male, soon followed by the other adults and finally the youngsters, as many as thirteen altogether. As I watched, over the lemon tree they came, the lead monkey testing the branches ahead of him to be sure they would bear his weight. When most of them were still crossing, he hopped into the second papaya and then saw my rope. I held my breath. He was no more than ten feet from where I sat. He lowered himself to where the rope was tied around his tree. He reached out to touch it. He held it in his hand for a little while, then he pulled on it. When it resisted his pull, he crossed in four skips to the third papaya tree, where he had never been before. Watching him think through his decision was fascinating enough, but even more so was watching the rest of the family follow him over the rope bridge as if it had always been there. Their constant stripping of the new growth finally killed those papaya trees, but it was worth it to get that close-up view of simian thought.

We all looked forward to Evelio's tomatoes behind the construction site, until I caught Koki spraying them with Malathion one day. I asked him what he was doing. "Protecting them from the birds," came the answer.

"And you want to poison the birds?" I asked.

He looked sheepishly at his feet. I don't know how many times I've told him over the years that Malathion is absorbed by the plant and makes it poisonous. The label, which Koki can't read – and neither could most literate people because the print is indecipherably small and the language is written by lawyers – says that the product is toxic and advises not to harvest the fruit of a plant sprayed with Malathion for two weeks after spraying. It's also absorbed by the skin, and I tell Koki to wear protective gear when he uses this or any other carcinogenic chemical, but he thinks it's macho to ignore the danger and so usually does it when I'm not looking. This is totally crazy, not to mention self-destructive, but I'm dealing with a person with not even a second-grade education, and I have found to my frustration over many years that this makes a boundary between us that simply won't be crossed.

There are other ways in which Koki displays his stubbornness. I found out about one of them the other day when Evelio and I were walking the fence-line. A number of posts were so rotten that any passing cow could just topple the fence and cross over. In fact, we found a small mound of cow manure that proved one of them already had. When we saw Koki with the weed-whacker a few moments later, I told him it was necessary to get after that fence right away. I knew he'd soon be taking his vacation, and I didn't want any cows invading when there was no Koki to chase them away. Tight-lipped, he turned away from me and stalked off.

I asked Evelio, "Is he angry at me?"

Evelio shrugged.

Later in the day, Koki found me writing up the day's events in my office and we talked about the fence situation at length. It turned out he hadn't been angry at me, but at our neighbor.

When we bought that strip of land – roughly 36 yards by 218 – it was to give us additional protection from what we thought was going to be a large residential development on the adjoining property. I spoke to the owner at the time and she verbally agreed to share the cost of a new fence; there were cows on the property, and as local custom has it, first, people share the cost and maintenance of fencing on mutual boundaries and, second, anyone with cows is responsible to keep them enclosed. This latter responsibility was recently codified into law. The custom, however, has been codified into the local ethic, such that new fences are always built half-and-half; that is, for one half of the distance the barbed wire is strung on one side of the posts and, for the other half, it's strung on the opposite side. In this way, I can point to "my fence," the upkeep for which I am responsible. In fact, owners usually agree to build their half-fence themselves, which means the quality can vary over the length of a fence. For this reason, I suggested to my neighbor that I have Koki and Evelio build a good, strong fence, and said I would let her know when it was done what her share of the cost would be. When it was all finished – 218 yards' worth, with the wire shifting from my side to hers at the 109-yard mark – I called to tell her the cost of materials and labor. She refused to pay.

Since I had no legal recourse at that time – there had been no written contract – I simply decided that I wasn't obligated to be nice to her, and I left it at that. Koki, on the other hand, took secret umbrage, and for years he has refused to touch my neighbor's half of that fence. She hasn't touched it either. In fact, she has done absolutely nothing to keep the cows from wandering onto our property, and every time they do, Koki now chases them out into the road, where they are legally vulnerable to police capture and slaughter – which so far hasn't happened, at least not around here.

It was my hope to let that entire strip of ground go wild, thus creating a naturally reforested barrier between us and our neighbor's property. So, until Evelio and I went searching for a place to plant his *frijol tapado,* I had never *seen* our neighbor's half of the fence and had no way of knowing its state of disrepair. I didn't get angry at Koki for this, although I contemplated speaking to him about what I saw as disrespect in his stalking off as he had done. After we talked, however, and I realized how personally he had taken the whole fence business – on our behalf! – there was no way I could reprimand him for his rudeness.

The next morning, Koki went over and talked to the man now leasing the property for his dairy operation. My thought was that the renter might be able to pressure the owner to fix the fence. But it turns out that the obligation to keep the fence in good repair is part of the lease, and the dairyman was very agreeable. He and Koki walked it together, in fact, and he said he would keep the cows out of that section until he could get to it. *Vamos a ver,* as they say around here. We'll see.

I became a citizen of Costa Rica in 2002. There were many reasons for this (none accepted by my father, who thought I was crazy). But one was that I wanted to "give back" to the country that was daily reminding me of my humanity, and I saw this could be done principally by working to protect the Arenal watershed. Most people don't know that this was declared a RAMSAR (International Convention on Wetlands) site many years ago, or that more recently it was recognized by UNICEF as part of one of the most important watersheds in Central America. Because of the lack of local regulation and oversight, big-money developers have been walking all over the country's environmental laws and threatening to turn Lake Arenal into a condo haven, bulldozing habitat as they go.

I was never an activist, until I lived in Costa Rica. The first time I saw a six-foot-diameter tree on the ground, illegally felled, my head fully understood all the economic reasons for cutting that tree down, but my heart refused to see how any human being could have done it. Unregulated development, especially here on the lake, has been personally painful to watch, and along with others I have worked hard to get government institutions to start paying attention. If I were not a citizen, I could be at risk of deportation. Big money can buy anything.

But there are other reasons. Over time I have found that every time I return to the United States, I feel more and more estranged, to the point where *it* now is the foreign country and Costa Rica, being more familiar, is home. From a distance it's much easier to get a broader picture of the place you have grown up and lived for most of your life. South of the border, one's perspective changes with exposure to other views. It's reached the point now where politically, socially, and even culturally, there's no way I could go back. It's hard to express this to people still living there, or even to people recently arrived for whatever reasons of their own. Living in another culture for a while begins to strip you of your native culture until you feel naked, as vulnerable as a baby, and you start to rethink the entire context in which you have lived your life. Given over twenty years of this battering – almost always kind here in Costa Rica – I have come to the conclusion that my innermost values are more closely aligned with what I have found here. Discovering something like that brings a peace one might never have expected. So, in this third age of my life, as difficult as some of the passages have been, I have to reflect that I have become a much happier human being.

People ask me if it was tough to get Costa Rican citizenship. I don't remember any particular difficulty with the paperwork – *trámites* – all ably managed by the lawyer who had handled my residency renewals. But I do remember – vividly! – the exams, one in Spanish and the other in history/civics/geography – for both of which I studied intensely for six weeks with the help of a couple of local high school teachers, and both of which were damned difficult. A happy byproduct of all that studying, however, was my discovery that I could actually learn to read in Spanish simply by doing it. I had been lazy about reading up to that point, but if I was going to meet the exam deadline there was no time to go to the dictionary every time I encountered a word I didn't know.

The other question people ask is, "But you could still keep your U.S. citizenship, no?"

I attended a ladies' luncheon once where a State Department wife looked around at us locals and asked, "So what brought you to Costa Rica?" and our outrageously candid neighbor Helen blurted out, "Monica Lewinsky!" I found this wonderfully comical, because the State Department wife was so obviously taken aback, and I couldn't help laughing out loud and saying, "That's it!"

If that puts me in a certain political camp, so be it. When my lawyer asked me if I intended to renounce my U.S. citizenship, I barely hesitated before saying yes. It just seemed to make every bit of sense to me at the time. My values had changed; my perspective on the U.S. had changed; the totality of my life – my heart – was here. So, I simply chose not to pursue dual citizenship and swore an act of renunciation in a tiny, bare interrogation room – yes, really – at the U.S. Embassy.

One of the tropical features of this house is the pyramid-shaped roof, peaked by a skylight over the atrium, lifted up a few inches and overhanging the roof tiles far enough that the rain can't get in. The openings under the four sides of the skylight were designed to work like a chimney in hot weather, pulling cool air into the house and forcing the warm air up and out. We never need air-conditioning; in fact, we almost never need to use a fan, and there are none installed in the ceilings. But in cold like this, the Trade Winds swoop past this super-ventilation system and drag any possible warmth our bodies have generated right out of the house. I have lived in the north and conscientiously turned the thermostat down to a barely livable 67 degrees Fahrenheit. This is colder. There are air-leaks around the doors. We never thought we'd need insulated glass in the windows. We are going to have to talk about winterizing.

This morning I appeared in the *bodega* in a fleece jacket with a beret pulled over my ears, and Evelio – also hatted and jacketed – greeted me with the single word, *hielo* – ice. I asked him when it was going to start snowing. I'm pretty sure it's not just my imagination that these Decembers are getting colder. All the locals agree it's never been this bad. The gringo neighbor who jokes, "Whatever happened to global warming?" isn't funny. One of the reasons I want to write these things down is to be able to look back in future years and compare to "what it was like then."

I am giving Roger a thermometer for Christmas. This runs counter to all my years of bragging, "Why do we need a thermometer? The temperature in Costa Rica never varies by more than 20 degrees!" A thermometer made sense in the north. It told you what to wear when you went out. It told you when you were freezing to death. Here I have never felt the need for one, until now.

Yesterday while the sun was briefly out, I strolled down the hill past the bananas we planted when we started building the house. Suddenly a big old toucan sailed out of one of them and I thought, aha, that bird is eating my bananas. Sure enough. Moving around the trees to get a better view through the long, flat leaves, I spotted a bunch of bananas half-eaten from the top down. Not only that, there were three other banana bunches on nearby trees not yet attacked by the birds, and I am determined to get them. Tomorrow I will speak to Koki about harvesting them. I know he is working hard to get the place "clean" – no weeds, no high grass – before he takes off for Christmas vacation. This means he's using the weed-whacker almost eight hours straight day after day until I think I will go crazy with the noise. He wears protective gear, including industrial-strength earmuffs, and I notice that wearing protective gear when whacking weeds is different from wearing protective gear while spraying carcinogenic chemicals. Wielding a $700 machine with all the proper paraphernalia is apparently a status thing. He sings *rancheras* at the top of his lungs as he whacks back and forth across the lawn. This includes the entire reforestation area in the old pasture, which he likes to think of as his park (he has told me more than once that people have stopped on the road to admire his work). So his eyes are on the ground, not on the bananas. I don't look forward to the day when I have to explain to him that it's a *forest* out there and he has to leave it alone, period.

Before he left for vacation, Koki walked the entire fence-line again to satisfy himself that all was secure, and no cows would invade for the week that he'd be gone. He came back to tell me he'd seen deer in the scrub that Evelio and I had been investigating for his *frijol tapado*. We knew they were in there, but it was wonderful to have this confirmation. Perhaps the small white-tailed deer are so magical to me because they're so difficult to see. One day, not long after Koki and Roger had conspired to clear the land that later became Evelio's garden, I saw a doe and two fawns feeding there. I was standing at the kitchen sink, and I held my breath in wonder – and in fear that the dogs would get onto them. But nothing disturbed them and they moved leisurely on into the scrub.

This morning, Evelio noted that the deer have been eating his bean plants. "But this is okay," he rushed to tell me before I could express my concern. "The deer are more important. This is an *ecological* garden." He has tacked up a couple of plastic bags that will rattle in the wind and discourage them.

This entire exercise is beginning to make me understand at close hand the potential conflicts between man and Nature. Because I can afford to buy vegetables at the market, I favor the deer over the beans in Evelio's garden. But when there aren't any vegetables in the market, what then? To some around here, deer is meat, necessary protein, and we occasionally hear guns in the wilderness between our property and the lake. It is a sad sound. The need for food is largely responsible for the alarming shrinkage of the Amazon rain forest, the lungs of the planet. And not just there, but everywhere in the world where poor people and trees and other species are locked in the grim competition for life.

The other day I walked out to the garden to say hello to Evelio, who was surveying with satisfaction his five thousand bean plants – black, white, and two kinds of red – and I asked him how he was going to spend Christmas. Mass on Christmas Eve, he told me, followed by a large gathering at his mother's house (all seven brothers, and even his father who hasn't lived with his mother for decades, plus various aunts and uncles and a sister-in-law and nieces and nephews) for tamales and coffee and *el calor navideño* (Christmas cheer). I liked that idea. Right now, only a lot of people huddled together in a small space will generate enough warmth for me. So we will do the same, only with friends – our adopted family – around a good meal and the small, live Christmas tree that we buy from my friend Tere's nursery.

Just before Christmas, I saw Koki with an armload of banana leaves for wrapping his wife's tamales. They were so perfectly rolled up and tied with a skinny strip of leaf that they could have been ready for sale in the local market. I was reminded of the essential sustainability of the old *campesino* lifestyle in Costa Rica; there was a use for everything, and everything grew back.

The extra-rich biodiversity of Costa Rica includes amoebas, one species of which has been bugging me off and on for several months. Each time, it seems to take a different medicine to rid me of the thing, which means the process drags out over several weeks during which eating is just a plain chore. As I do every Christmas morning, I visited a few local families to swap out homemade gingerbread for tamales, and at one house I happened to mention my amoeba. Alba, mother of three, said she had cured one of her boys of an amoeba recently with the bark of the olive tree – *la cáscara de aceituno*. Her husband, Mariano, volunteered to take me to a nearby farm where he could whack off some more of this bark with his machete. The farmer came out to greet us. He was pleased to offer the bark of his tree if it would make the *señora* feel better. While Mariano trekked downhill to the tree, I waited at the edge of the pasture in the weak sunlight, observing the makeshift rusty tin-roofed sheds and cheap plastic plumbing fittings around me, smelling the cow manure, realizing that this poor family had been on this land for a long time, cluttering up the farmyard in whatever ways necessary to house and care for their chickens and pigs and cows. There were a few scraggly fruit trees dotting the landscape, just as abandoned as ours. Mariano snagged an orange from one as he came back up the hill.

I read in the paper the other day that the cost to produce a *tamal* has gone up by 30 percent this year. Mariano's family is indeed poor, so to spare four *tamales* to give to me is a stretch. The only additional gift they can give is their time and care, so I was keenly aware, as I waited for Mariano on that poor farm, that this was truly a Christmas moment.

The next day, Friday, I called the doctor to tell him the current medication was not only not working, it was causing severe gastric distress. He was not disposed to see me until late Monday, nor did he have any suggestions for an alternate medication. This annoyed me enough to try the *cáscara de aceituno,* so I asked Rosa how to prepare it. She had heard of it too, as a cure for not only amoebas but a whole lot of other *bichos*.

I stood at the kitchen counter and watched her pull out a pot big enough to accommodate my gift from Mariano and Alba. She plunked everything into the pot with water to cover and commenced boiling. It boiled for a long time. As we waited, she told me that her parents were finally getting married. I expressed surprise that, in all the years I have known Rosa, I never knew her parents *weren't* married. Of course, under Costa Rican law, their union is certainly legal after 50 years of living together and raising a family. But for Rosa, the religious tie is more important than the common law. She said her father always joked that he was waiting for just the right fifteen-year-old. Now that he is dying of stomach cancer, he has finally agreed to tie the knot. Rosa said her mother was so excited that her blood pressure hit the ceiling and she had to be rushed off to the clinic. I laughed and said, "Let's hope she makes it to Friday!" That's the day the priest is coming to the house, since neither bride nor groom is well enough to go to the church. Rosa said they weren't inviting anybody, but that everybody in the village is coming anyway, some with food, others with music. This is Evelio's village too, so he'll be there.

After the infusion had cooled, Rosa strained the dark liquid into a jar, telling me to take a tablespoonful first thing in the morning for eight days. What the hell.

Another Christmas morning tradition is visiting José Adémar and his wife, Ana, and this year I reminded Adémar of our conversation so many years ago about living off the land. We had been speaking of politics, the economy, and climate change, and I was gratified to see he remembered our old conversation very well. He told me that the big wind last January took out half of his macadamia trees. He's planting beans.

It is interesting to me that not a single Costa Rican I know has any doubts about global warming, while there are still so many in the North who deny it altogether. It must be that living close to the land predisposes one to the idea that human beings are an integral part of the ecosystem and that we can, in fact *do*, damage it in countless ways.

At dawn now I am hearing the Laughing Falcon, for the first few days, a solitary, and now a pair. I would love to see this bird, a new arrival to our farm in just the last two years, but like many other birds of prey, they're hard to see up close. Their loud call, however, is like nothing else. The locals call them *guacos,* because of the "series of loud, rhythmic hollow *wha* notes that gradually increase in pitch and loudness, finally breaking into a series of *wha'-co* phrases, the entire sequence lasting a minute or more" (according to *A Guide to the Birds of Costa Rica,* Stiles & Skutch, 1989, hereinafter The Bird Book). This morning, curling up under the covers until the sun came up, I heard a duet. Is it too early for a mating pair? The Bird Book says "dry season," so perhaps this pair is getting ready. One indigenous tradition holds that if a pair of *guacos* sings in a green tree we will have rain; if in a dry tree, dry weather.

Earlier this year, Koki told me he saw up to a hundred nests in the new trees in the reforestation zone/park. We had planted these only a few years before, so it was thrilling to discover that our little reforestation project was already home to more wildlife. We've reforested on the other side of the *quebrada* too, as well as in the strip of land Evelio and I were exploring the other day. All these extra trees are attracting more birds, and this must at least partially account for the presence of species we have never seen before. Scientists talk about how species are already migrating uphill as global temperatures rise. What happens when they get to the top? Roger's answer to that question, which he tells everybody we know, as well as all the tourists he runs into, is "plant more trees."

January
Cow Wars

The fence story is far from over. I assumed that the dairyman renting next door figured up the cost of fifty fence posts and carried off his cows under cover of night, because we started seeing animals we didn't recognize breaching the fence. No, *breach* is too mild a verb. They were simply walking over it, since most of the posts are lying on the ground. Two horses one day. A bull the next. A cow *and* the same black bull the next. I told Koki to catch the bull and cow and tie them to a post out on the road, and I called the police. Historically, the *Guardia Rural* resolved these kinds of questions, coming out to the property, looking at the fence, and reminding both owners of their responsibilities under the law. No more. The Rural Guard is now called the *Fuerza Pública* (Public Force) and so far I haven't been able to figure out what their new duties are, aside from riding around town in their new blue Daihatsu patrol car. Over the years, we have contributed generously every time they've come around asking for money (always for car parts), but they seem to have forgotten us. They referred me to the municipal civil court. Nothing doing there either. I used to know the people there well, as I had to go in every month to sign for my alimony checks. But that was years ago, and now a different woman at the desk tells me I can't even file a complaint myself – I have to go to a lawyer.

Propelled by my anger at my neighbor and my increasing frustration, I drove over to the office of our lawyer, Willy. He and his brother, Alvaro, are the sharpest lawyers in town, as well as owners of considerable cattle

67

lands. Neither of them needs to lawyer at all; Alvaro once confessed to me that he does it for the sheer fun of it. Willy is also the drummer in a rock band.

Willy was surprised that the police had been unable to help. That would have been the simplest way of handling the problem. Without them, we had to go to the criminal court in Cañas. For this, I needed various papers that I had to unearth from the safe deposit box at the bank and from the municipal *catastro* office – where they now have everybody's properties beautifully accessible on computer. The lines on the computer maps look so comforting and solid, whereas the truth on the ground is anything but. Nothing is easy in Costa Rica, or even if you speak the language and have a pocketful of patience. Everything always comes back to patience.

Meanwhile, the bull escaped, and I told Koki to put the cow in the reforestation lot on the other side of the *quebrada*. I didn't want anybody driving by to steal the evidence. Unfortunately, the owner of the cow showed up this morning looking for his missing heifer. We had to confess that we had her, and so the evidence has gone. He was a bit chagrined to find that the fence was in such poor condition and that we have been routinely chasing his animals out onto the road where – another little tidbit of Costa Rican law – if they get into an accident with a car, he would be responsible for all damages.

Cows are really very stupid animals. I have never liked them. They walk the same paths day in and day out, year in and year out, wearing the ground down into deep gullies that crisscross the hillsides and erode in the torrential rains, sending avalanches plummeting downwards. They expel methane and, in the numbers that populate the giant feedlots in the north, they are a serious contributor to global warming. Cows are no respecters of fences. They are motivated by only one idea in their tiny brains, and that is that whatever is on the *other* side of the fence is going to be better than what's on *this* side. So they push at the posts and shove their heads through the barbed wire trying to reach the tastiest treats, whether beans, forest seedlings, or just grass of a different color. Over time, they stretch the wire, loosen the staples, and knock down the posts. We have chased cows all over the lawn, Roger has sling-shot marbles at them, the dogs have bitten their legs, and *still* they come. We have been fighting cows ever since we have lived on this land, trying to be good neighbors, fixing the fences ourselves, never insisting on our rights. *Now* is going to be different. And I have to prepare myself for the probability that this will take a long, long time.

Thank God you don't have to be divorced in Costa Rica to receive an alimony check, because within months of our "good faith" separation agreement, my former husband had reneged because I was seeing Roger, and my meager, but livable, portion suddenly stopped. That's when things turned ugly, and I was forced to sue him for a *pension alimenticia* (literally, food pension). My husband showed up before the local magistrate – at nine in the morning – drunk.

"What's your name?" he gurgled to the judge. In this country, "name" means first name.

The judge answered, "Juan."

"Hello, Juan," my husband went on. "Do you like to fish?"

My eyes were glued to the floor. I was awarded 250 dollars less than what I had been getting. I was living as frugally as I could, with no phone or car, but I had my mare pastured in the fields behind me. On Sunday mornings I would ride around to the local villages and say hello to people.

I turned myself to whatever work I could find, but

quickly my vet friend Eric got in touch with his sister-in-law, who was director of a prestigious language school, and the next thing I knew I was giving adult night classes in English in Tilarán. That's the way things happen in Costa Rica. I didn't have the job long – the institute decided to abandon Tilarán – but I got some valuable training.

I coordinated with my divorce lawyer in San José via the post office fax machine and in the phone booth in front of the parochial hall (the cord just long enough to allow me to sit on the sidewalk going over long documents line by line), with an occasional four-and-a-half-hour bus trip into the city, while my soon-to-be former husband did his best to malign my character, terrify me with slow midnight cruises back and forth in front of my house honking his horn (I knew he owned a gun), and leave filthy letters in my P.O. box, copies of which he would fax to my parents in Florida. Costa Rica didn't then have the protections against harassment and domestic violence that are now codified into law. At one point, I was frightened enough to move down to the beach, where Roger had taken a three-month job fixing up a few *cabinas*.

My removal from the situation helped to calm things down, but it took two years and the threat of a suit for financial fraud to bring my husband finally to the negotiating table. During all that time, I kept my focus: I was going to stay in Costa Rica and I was going to get clarity about what had gone on during the previous fifty years, so that I wouldn't repeat any of it. This took a lot of determination and a lot of writing – notebook after notebook – but when it was all over, I felt free, cleansed, and already embarked on a new life.

On the second day of the year, I walked down through

Koki's Park to see the *ceiba* tree. Roger asked me if I'd seen it lately, and I hadn't. The trees between the house and the *ceiba* have grown up so much that the foliage blocks the view. Roger was right: it's huge. At shoulder-level I could just touch my fingers around its girth. I walked around it amazed. Carved into the trunk a little below eye-level were three names: *Danilo*, *Silenia* and *Evelio*, the latter with the date of *March 9, 2008*.

I came back up to the house filled with pleasure, because I had planted that *ceiba* from seed, and I wanted to find out from Koki just when we had put the seedling in the ground. Together we worked out that it had been sometime in 2003, which means I planted the seed at least a year earlier, when our friend Ed invited me to tromp around his mother's farm. It was there under a giant specimen that I had found a partially opened seed pod with the kapok peeking through. Picking through the silky threads to free the seeds was a chore and, of all the seeds I planted in plastic pots, only one took hold. It's now the tallest thing around.

There is something about the *ceiba*, with its massive trunk, buttresses and heavy branches arching out from the crown, that invokes simple awe. It's easy to understand why the Maya considered it sacred. They called it the First Tree, or World Tree, and they believed it to be standing at the center of the Earth. The *ceiba* can reach a venerable age – 400 years and more. There's one on the other side of Tilarán that measures 33 feet across, with buttresses higher than a house. *Ceibas* are fast growers, and in their first few years they throw out large sharply pointed spikes to keep predators at bay. Our *ceiba* has lost most of its spikes, except for a few down at ground level. I look forward to the development of its first buttresses, necessary for a shallowly rooted tropical tree that has to bear so much weight. It's already obvious that this tree is braving the full force of the winds; most of its branches are on the leeward side.

I asked Koki: who, aside from Evelio, had carved their names in the smooth bark? It was his second son, Hairo Danilo, and his sister-in-law. Why the *ceiba?* I thought to ask him. He said people believe that the *ceiba* is one of only a few species that preserve the letters close to each other as the tree grows in girth. So marking a *ceiba* is like leaving a legacy; your name will last forever. Roger and I like to think that *planting* a *ceiba* is leaving a legacy, too.

The *guachepelín* trees are in bloom, their brilliant yellow flowers visible from miles away. The tiny petals, dislodged by the wind, swirl and collect along the roadsides, making me think of streets paved with gold. *Gua* is an ancient indigenous word meaning "tree," and it still survives in many names in Costa Rica, including the *guanacaste,* which is the national tree. I love the *guachepelín* for its twisty shape and rough bark. It makes a good bonsai, because the bark quickly takes on an ancient look and the tortured architecture of the branches also contributes to a sense of age. When José Adémar was building the house for my parents, I said I wanted "natural" posts to support the verandah roof, and he suggested *guachepelín.* He pointed out that we had several of these trees on the lot, although none was old enough to serve the purpose. He found some beautiful specimens elsewhere, and their tortured shapes were certainly striking along the length of that verandah. It was only later I learned that the *guachepelín,* like so many other tropical hardwoods, is endangered. By that time I had discovered my passion for *living* trees.

Yesterday I was accompanied through my entire half-hour exercise routine on the verandah by a single male *zanate* (Great-tailed grackle) in the *guanacaste* tree. These birds are ubiquitous and not very nice, as one of their food strategies is stealing eggs from other birds' nests. In the trees of central parks all over Costa Rica, they settle down at dusk by the thousands, kicking up an ungodly racket. Municipalities try in vain to get rid of them. Tilarán cut down all the beautiful *ficus* trees in our park, under the mistaken notion that the *zanates* prefer roosting in this species. The birds roosted in the almond trees instead, and there was no discernable diminution in either their numbers or the noise.

My friend Francisco, local legend and songwriter, now deceased, wrote a ballad about the *zanates* in the park in Cañas keeping the secrets of the young lovers trysting there in the evenings. I wish I had written down the words; it was my favorite of his songs.

I like the *zanates,* in spite of their bad habits. The glossy blue-black males strut self-importantly across the lawn; the females gaggle together as if they had just met up at the mall. Most of all, I love their vocal pyrotechnics.

On the exercise bike, I pump away to an ancient cassette of the Bee Gees on an equally ancient Walkman plugged into my ears. Yesterday the Bee Gees were losing to a noisy *zanate* in the *guanacaste* tree. I had to laugh at all the variations he was producing: chirps, cheeps, clicks, clacks, clucks, chatters, chuckles, rattles, slides, screeches, toots, trills, twitters, whistles, and warbles. There is truly no more versatile vocalist in Costa Rica.

In addition to the herbs out on the verandah, there is a proliferation of other plants, most of them gifts. This is part of the culture in the *campo,* swapping cuttings around. Since everything grows in the tropics, everyone here is a gardener. I don't know a single *tica* who doesn't have some specialty, be it orchids, hibiscus, roses, or cacti, and she is always delighted to show off her plants and offer the admirer a cutting or two. The Christmas cactus that has been blooming so beautifully right through the holidays was a gift from Olga, Koki's wife. The two-toned African violets (white with purple edges) came from Nidia, a neighbor of Rosa's in Sabalito; the pale lavender ones are from Alba, she of the recipe for my amoeba; Luis Diego provided the potted palms; and Rosa herself added the dwarf roses in three colors and the green and white caladium. There are bonsai as well – or I should say *attempts* at bonsai – some doing well and some reminding me of my negligence, and I have given plenty of them away. There is even a prehistoric-looking mystery plant from a cutting Roger brought back from southern California.

For a number of years, I was blessed with a gardener named Rafa, who knew more about gardening than anyone I have ever met, which in a country of gardeners is saying a lot. He could chew the leaf of a citrus tree and tell you whether it was a lime, sweet or sour lemon, grapefruit, tangerine, or any of a dozen varieties of orange. He knew propagation from graft, cutting, seed. He recognized blights, fungi, damaging insects, knew when something in the soil was making a plant *triste* (sad). He knew all the medicinal uses of everything in the garden, and he was always carting off leaves and sticks to neighbors for their stomachs or their nerves. I would argue with Rafa about the pruning; if there was a fruit or a seed on a branch, he wouldn't cut it. Gardening in Costa Rica has a lot to do with food. When he did prune something, the cuttings would go back into the garden, and in less-trodden places I would come across whole rows of yellow crotons or giant-flowering hibiscus that had been started from the results. I lived in fear of the luxuriant tropical growth completely engulfing the house and would, myself, go out hacking with a machete in a vain effort at control. The real challenge with gardening in Costa Rica is finding – and keeping – a balance so that your yard looks like a garden instead of a jungle.

Here on the verandah I started with only two African violets and now have ten. If a leaf breaks off when Rosa is dusting around them, she sticks it in a pot. Nothing should ever go to waste.

Local wisdom has it that the *heat* creates earthquakes. Koki reminded me of this after the killer 6.2 quake the other day along a deep fault line between Poás and Barva Volcanoes that sent huge sections of mountainside thundering into the valley below, sweeping houses and people and cattle with it. According to Koki, day after day of unrelenting sun beating down on the earth causes it to tremble. Having heard this theory before, I simply nodded.

It does not take much to remind us that where education fails, country wisdom takes over. Until the current generation, few people in our area made it through the sixth grade. Even among the young people we know, most have had only a year or two of high school. Rural family economics means taking children out of school as soon as they are of a reasonable age to work – Koki went to work at nine – so there's a lot they miss, including the very interesting geology of a country that sits on top of three converging tectonic plates.

I shared Koki's view with Roger later in the day, and he harrumphed at the persistence of local ignorance. I pointed out that all it takes to reinforce such lore is a once-in-a-decade quake at the beginning of the warmer dry season. In Costa Rica, this happens all the time.

I like looking out the kitchen window at the rows and rows of bean plants, all so bright and neatly ordered. Except for a sizeable plot of cilantro and a tiny area of carrots, the whole 66-by-33-yard field is beans, beans and more beans. I walked the rows yesterday and noted that Evelio hasn't thinned the carrots. He never thinned the radishes either. On every seed packet I have ever read, it says to thin when the sprouts have reached a certain size. I mentioned this to Evelio when the radishes were coming in, but he ignored it. (Is this machismo or simply his perception that I'm not an "expert"?) So the carrots coming in are all jammed together, and we'll see what percentage of the crop he loses.

I pulled one up, and it was a poor carrot indeed. I now firmly suspect that there will be no planting and tending of vegetables until the wind dies down in May, and he begins spending less time at the windsurf center.

Incredibly, in mid-January, the first flowers are showing up on the *corteza amarillo,* the noble old tree right against the south side of the house. These blossoms are truly an energized yellow that makes the *guachepelín* blooms pale by comparison. It's an old tree. Some years it flowers vigorously and some years it doesn't. Last year was spectacular, so we'll see what this year brings. You only see single *cortezas* around the countryside, never in groves. This species, too, is endangered. I'll ask Koki to keep a close look out for seeds again this year.

The day after I got home from San José, Koki rescued a kitten from the dogs. I got the full story a day later when I took the phone bill over to Joe, the surfboard shaper renting the little house. He had been cooking bacon and eggs when the kitten jumped up on the kitchen window. He went outside and pulled it off the screen before it could do any damage, then took it out to the road and told it to get along. Undaunted, kitty followed Joe back to the house and, when he opened the door, darted in ahead of him. "Nothing doing," said Joe, and he scooped up the kitten and took it back outside and perched it in the crotch of a tree. At this point the dogs got interested, and Koki came running to see what they were barking at. Koki rescued the kitten and brought it to Roger in his downstairs man cave/office, where it lived and ate ravenously for two and a half days until some cat-loving friends agreed to adopt it. We guessed it was about five weeks old. Someone had dropped it off, obviously figuring the gringos would take care of it. It was probably one of several; I'm assuming the others didn't survive.

This dropping off of animals is nothing new. *All* of our animals in Costa Rica – with the exception of my mare – were abandoned in one way or another. Fortuna was rescued from the streets of Tilarán by our friend Eric, the head of animal health at the local office of the Ministry of Agriculture. Knowing our previous three dogs had recently been poisoned (since the drug cartels' recent incursions into Costa Rica, burglaries are up, but our house is difficult to burgle, so those three deaths were for nothing), Eric called to see if I'd be willing to take care of a street dog and her two puppies over the weekend, since he had to go to

San José and there would be nobody in the office to feed her. I suspected that he was trying to get rid of a problem and, sure enough, after dropping off our next set of three dogs, he never called me back. We found a home for one of the puppies. The other had to be put down because she developed encephalitis. Fortuna, the mother, remained.

While all this was going on, somebody dropped off two puppies at the windsurf center. Roger started feeding them, and they became the latest "windsurf dogs," until one was run over by a tourist-mobile that broke the puppy's femur and shattered its off-side elbow. That dog had to be put down too. With Fortuna now by herself, we decided to bring the other windsurf puppy over to the house to keep her company. There is now a new windsurf dog that Evelio rescued from his village of Río Piedras. When the dust settled, we realized we had buried five dogs in the pet cemetery within little more than a month.

Any poor country will be hard on pets. People don't have the money to vaccinate, neuter or even feed them properly. This is especially true for cats, who are usually expected to feed themselves. Then there are the dangers of the wild, such as boa constrictors, hawks, and vehicles on the road. (Our friend Roberta hacked up a boa with her machete to free a cat it had started to swallow, but she was too late.) There is also ehrlichia, a tick-borne bacterium that eats away at a dog's immune system until it dies of anemia or a secondary infection. We learned about that one the hard way, and now we are especially attentive to possible early symptoms, such as a slight lack of energy or an intermittent limp. In Fortuna's case, recently, I noticed that she'd stopped jumping up on my clean blue jeans. When we took her to the vet her leucocytes were less than half normal levels, so we put both dogs on doxycycline for twenty-two days. A vet we know in Puntarenas estimates that 90 percent of the dogs there are infected. Tick bites dog, then carries the infection to the next dog, *ad infinitum*. Here the numbers don't seem to be as drastic, but the first line of defense, obviously, has to be tick control – difficult to do in the *campo*.

A few years ago, vet Eric and a friend of his, Judy, invited me to help start up a nonprofit that would raise money to do spay/neuter clinics in poor communities as a way to control the abandoned pet population. When the Guanacaste Province Animal Welfare Foundation first offered these clinics, local people were skeptical; we were lucky to draw thirty animals in a day. Now that number has more than doubled, and people are begging us to come to their villages. Statistically, euthanasia – as practiced in traditional animal shelters or municipal pounds – doesn't have much of an impact on the unwanted pet population. Animals just seem to breed faster. Neutering every animal you can get your hands on is the only solution, but even with the more than two thousand animals the foundation has already done, there are hundreds and hundreds more just in our *cantón* alone. At some point, though, a critical mass is reached, and the population starts to stabilize. In a few of the villages where the foundation has worked, this has already happened.

I noticed the first black raspberries have popped out on the vine that Koki has supported with a neat trellis of bamboo. They're not ripe yet, but I could see that some of the ones near ground-level had already been eaten. This was a mystery to me – why would the birds go after them from the bottom up? – until Koki told me that Fortuna likes them! I wonder how she picks them without getting her nose stuck by the thorns.

Koki said we have a pair of *chompipes* in the *quebrada*. I pulled out the Bird Book so he could identify them for me – the Crested Guan. *Chompipe* is another word for turkey, and there are several in this bird family in Costa Rica, although this one, at under four pounds (1.7kilos) certainly doesn't conjure up images of Thanksgiving dinner. I asked him if they were new here, and he said yes, this is the first year he has seen them on the property. He thought they might have been attracted by the corn that our neighbor Renate puts down for her domestic flock up the hill. But the book also says these guans are forest birds, that they have disappeared from deforested parts of the country and that they are even "becoming rare in unprotected forests." It thrills me once again to realize that we are recreating habitat here. It's an invitation: *See what a nice house we are building for you? Why don't you move in!*

Recently one of Renate's turkeys flew out of its enclosure and across the road onto our land. Fortuna had it by the neck in a flash – she is fleeter than many birds – but Koki rescued it before any real damage was done and returned it to its owner. A previous escapee wasn't so lucky. Another one-time windsurf dog chased that turkey into the brush and killed it before I could get to it. She also ate it. I never told anyone.

The *laureles* are flowering – not many on our farm yet, but they are beginning to burst forth around the countryside between here and Tilarán. There are lots of *laurel* trees in the reforestation ground on the other side of the *quebrada,* where somebody surely planted them for lumber years ago. When they're in full bloom, their billowing white canopies, all converging along the *quebradas* or in the wood lots, look like mountains of improbable snow in the tropical landscape. With their tall, slender trunks, these showy trees remind me of delicate Japanese scroll paintings, all black and white and shades in between.

At the end of the last day in January, a blustery day driving chill-heavy rains across the lake, Koki brought me a *zapote*. It was hard and grainy and avocado-shaped, and he assured me that in a week it would be *muy rico,* very delicious. I have perched the fruit on the kitchen windowsill so I won't forget to check it now and then. When it softens a bit, I'll open it to see what's inside.

There is something Edenic about all this bounty growing so lushly everywhere year-round. One imagines that it would almost be possible to live without working, simply moving from tree-to-tree to satisfy one's hunger. I remember once marveling that I couldn't buy lemons at a local *pulpería.* "Wait a second," said the proprietor, as I huffed out my frustration. I was in the middle of a recipe that called for lemon juice and had dashed out to the local store to find one. I waited at the counter, tapping my toe on the cement floor, feeling hurried and out of control. How could a store not have lemons in a country literally loaded with them? A few minutes later, the owner came back bearing a plastic bag of lemons. "Wonderful!" I exclaimed. "How much do I owe you for these?" He demurred. He wasn't sure. "What do you mean?" I supposed he had pulled these out of the bodega at the back, and I was amazed he didn't remember how much he had paid for them. "I just picked them off the tree behind my house," he said.

In a country where lemons grow everywhere, why would anyone need to buy them at the store?

The Volcano

One of the reasons we built our house in the air was to ensure an unimpeded view of one of the most active volcanoes in the world.

When Roger first arrived in Costa Rica over 20 years ago, he came directly from the airport to a small rented house high above the lake. He dropped his windsurf gear on the porch and flopped into a handy hammock just in time to catch the incredible nighttime pyrotechnics of a full volcanic eruption. While he's lived in other houses since, he has never lived more than ten minutes away from a view of Volcán Arenal; we even had a small slice of view through the fence-line trees from the little house. In choosing the site up the slope for the new house, we picked the highest spot on the property and farthest from the road. Roger was so determined to make the main living floor of the house high enough for volcano viewing that he assembled our rickety scaffolding on the site as high as it would go, then positioned our tallest step ladder on top of that, and then climbed up to assure himself we would see the whole spectacular show. Descending with a satisfied grin, he invited me to climb up and see for myself, but I couldn't get past the top of the scaffolding (where I remained on my knees until I could gather the courage to climb back down).

So you would think the volcano has played a major role in our lives ... and it has, but only in the background. In all my years on the lake, I have never seen a nighttime fireworks display like the one Roger saw. I have seen it go off during the day - although now "sleeping," until 2010 it was sending up gases and pyroclastic material almost all the time. I always heard it first - a distant thudding *boom* -

and then I would turn to see the huge, ashy plume ascending skyward and, depending on the light and the direction of the flow, great smoky cascades rolling down its slopes. We're 22 miles away, more or less, from what the newspaper always calls "the colossus," and there were plenty of times – as when we were asleep – that we just didn't hear it. Our bedroom doesn't face it; if the wind is blowing, we don't hear it at all.

I look for it countless times during the day from the house and every time I drive into Tilarán. The lakeshore drive is one of the most scenic routes in Costa Rica and, between here and Cinco Esquinas two miles away, there are plenty of impressive long views of water and mountain, although the volcano is not always visible. Arenal makes its own weather and is often shrouded in clouds or mist. But even hidden, it holds a kind of sway over the imaginations of those of us who live near it, and we read every article about it in the paper as if it belonged to us personally.

Articles a few years ago in *La Nación* talked about how fast Arenal Volcano was *growing*. It was adding almost five meters (more than 16 feet) to its height every year, and the thickness of the walls of the main crater had grown between 12 and 18 meters since it had been measured a year earlier. The buildup of material was changing the contours of the mountain, redirecting eruptions to new territory. Discharged material – rocks, sand and ash – was exceeding what was once considered the footprint of the volcano on the ground and flows of up to 800 degrees Celsius were igniting ancient virgin forest in the national park. Paths once considered safe were no longer. Pyroclasts move a lot faster than lava – over 90 miles-per-hour fast.

There's no outrunning Arenal. When it blew in 1968, after 143 years of dormancy, 78 people and untold numbers of domestic and wild animals were killed. It was just farm country and small villages around a much smaller Arenal then. Now the area is a huge tourist attraction, with all the attendant services, and there are many, many more people at risk. We don't spend a lot of time over there, although if it ever blew as it did in 1968, we would not be immune, even at this distance and with the full length of the lake between us and the mountain. It was no Krakatoa, but Arenal's ash fell on Tilarán for weeks, as people migrated – in oxcarts, on horseback and on foot from east to west carrying the clothes on their backs and what they had hurriedly saved of their goods and animals. One man I talked to who had formed part of that dreary procession described the cloud hanging over the volcano as a "perfect cauliflower." I have also heard that, if the wind conditions were right, the gases alone from a major eruption would kill everything for miles around. So we should never be smug about how safe we are at the opposite end of the lake.

Arenal is a composite volcano, like Mount Fuji, producing eruptions of both lava and pyroclasts and with a similar conical shape, although Fuji is much older, so its sides are more gently sloped. I saw just the slopes of "Fuji-san" when I travelled on the bullet train from Tokyo to Kyoto many years ago. The so-familiar profile of the peak was hidden in cloud, just as Arenal often is. We have of one of that wonderful series of 19th-century woodblock prints by the great Japanese artist Hokusai called *36 Views of Mt. Fuji*. In most of these prints, the mountain doesn't star. Instead, you see scenes of Japanese life at the time, with sometimes just a hint of the volcanic profile in the distant background. This is how I see Volcán Arenal: sometimes a looming shadow, sometimes a conical mass of cloud, sometimes just a delicate line suspended eerily above a layer of mist. It's the background to our lives. We never forget it's there.

February
Evelio vs. Nature, Round Two

The first two days of the month couldn't have been lovelier. Everybody heaved a sigh of relief and nodded sagely to each other, saying the dry season had arrived at last, and not a minute too soon. On the third, we were hit by a freight-train wind driving heavy rains. "Where did this come from?" everyone was asking. "How can we be having this weather in *February*?"

Roger, who keeps track of the weather, announced on Monday afternoon when I got back from Liberia – what had been a long, hot, dusty trip of multiple errands – that a new storm was moving in that would bring high winds later in the week. Ha! During the night we were awakened when it hit, sounding like a baseball bat beating the bedroom wall. The skylight rattled, the chimney whooshed, the glass of the window above the bedstead felt icy. We threw on an extra blanket and hunkered under the covers with the cat. The next day, as I rounded the corner of the house to water plants on the verandah, I was nearly blown off my feet. Four days later at 6:30 a.m. it was 59 degrees Fahrenheit outside and 63 in. Does knowing this, now that we have this wonderful little thermometer, make it feel even colder?

Next to the house the great central trunk of the *corteza amarillo* that I've been waiting to see bloom snapped on Tuesday night, leaving just the lower branches still reaching out to the sky. I have feared for this tree in every heavy wind since we moved into the house; I know it's old. Now its heart is gone; just the exoskeleton remains.

With all the unusual rain (*more* flooding on the Caribbean side), the lake is again at its fullest. But that doesn't stop ICE (Instituto Nacional de Electricidad) from predicting energy rationing for the coming dry season. Everybody loves to hate ICE; along with politics and *fútbol,* hating the electricity and (up till recently) telephone monopoly is a national pastime. How we love to observe company employees spraying herbicides along the shore of the lake! How we envy those brand-new Toyota trucks they're all driving! How we screech when the phone service is out for five days!

Because of the hydro projects, Lake Arenal is ICE country. In fact, Tilarán bills itself as "the energy heart of Costa Rica." In addition to three hydro plants, there are multiple wind farms and, just northwest of here, several geothermal plants tapping into the steam under Miravalles Volcano. We're producing more energy around here than any other part of the country ... and we have more outages than anybody else. In fact, we love to brag about it.

The *zopilote* is a flying ace, cruising the thermals with seamless ease, barely lifting a feather to soar straight and true. I know it is hunting for carrion, but I'm also convinced it loves to fly. On the ground, a vulture is an ungainly thing. A group of them together tearing away at a roadkill makes me hold my breath as I drive by. But, as foul as they look when feeding, they keep the countryside clean and so play an important role in the ecosystem. In 50-mile-per-hour winds yesterday, I watched one struggle into the east, reeling, careening, sheering back and forth trying to gain a purchase, barely edging forward across the sky. There are windsurfers who exult in extreme conditions; for them life is a pitched battle against the elements. I don't think that vulture was having much fun out there yesterday; it looked too much like work.

Evelio was in a dark mood as I drove him into town this morning: no tourists at the windsurf center, and half his bean crop damaged by the wind. He said he had been hoping with this crop to make up all the expenses on his previous "failures." I asked him how much that was, and he responded with what seemed to me an astronomical figure.

"So much?" I asked incredulously.

"That includes my time," he said.

God only knows at what hourly rate he was hoping to reimburse himself. I didn't bother to ask him about *our* expenses. He was talking about taking a job on some farm, any farm, taking care of cattle or chickens, whatever. According to Roger, earlier in the week Evelio had been talking about getting back into construction (although now opportunities are slim). He's been making good money at the windsurf center for most of the season, just not in this awful weather. He's even managed to sock away enough in the new savings account Roger insisted he open to pay himself a basic salary for *forty weeks* of no windsurf clients at all. But all he sees is what's directly in front of his nose.

I was too dispirited myself today to try to talk Evelio out of his depression; instead, I focused on the warmth pumping out of the car heater. If the weather would warm up just a notch, we'd *all* feel better.

Roger relieved Evelio at the windsurf center this afternoon so he could run the new high-speed Internet cables under the floor. I was out on the verandah watering plants when he popped his head out my office door and said that looking at his bean field had made him "extremely desolate."

"This crop is a failure. I'm not going to plant anything here ever again. I have lost all hope," he wound up dramatically.

I suppose that if he'd hit me with this in the morning, I might have had more patience, but I had run around town for a couple of hours' worth of errands today and I was tired and a little exasperated by all the drilling and rearranging of furniture going on in my office. Not to mention that he never sweeps up after himself.

"Evelio, I have lost all patience with you! Every time you face a little obstacle, you abandon whatever project happens to be disappointing you, and I don't ever want to hear you say you have lost all hope again, when the world is going to hell in a handbasket and you're sitting here pretty with a good job and lots of skills and no fear of facing starvation!"

He ducked his head back through the door and I finished my watering and, finally, I came back inside and sat down and apologized for losing my temper.

Somehow, we got through it. The fact is that we are friends at a level deeper than these irritations. I am reminded of the time when Evelio was on the crew building our house. He managed to cut out all the windows on one side of the house an inch higher than on the other three sides. Roger was beside himself and must have given poor Evelio an earful. Evelio stalked down to the little house, where I was working on some lesson plans, to tell me he was quitting. I took one look at him, knew instantly that something truly terrible had happened, and was given the inspiration to say, just like his mother, "Evelio, how can you do this to me? I need you! Nobody else can do all the things you do. You can't leave!" He looked at me quizzically for a moment, then said "Okay," turned on his heel and went back to work.

Today I wanted to help him see the difference between a commercial bean crop and an experimental organic garden, between being in business for profit and enjoying as a pastime what he loves to do best, which is to play in the dirt and grow things. I reminded him that what "organic" essentially means is working *with* Nature, respecting its ways, accepting its conditions, learning how to thrive alongside it without doing it harm. If we can't grow beans in the windy season, then we let the plot go until conditions are better, or we plant something else that *can* withstand the wind. He got the idea, I think, because he suggested dwarf oranges! (I'm already wondering how much a hundred little grafted trees will cost.)

Let's hope that does it for a while.

We are having a one-day respite between cold fronts, and what a day it is! Tricksy, the yellow cat, and I had a brief schmooze this morning out on what I call the "sunning platform" – the place where the outside stair turns the corner, a lovely four-by-four-foot patch of pine decking that warms up beautifully on a sunny day. It was a blessed respite after I had walked out to the gate and observed some additional pruning I want Koki to do.

I have never been able to explain to Koki just what I mean by pruning. I was taught that, in order to make a shrub bushy, it needs to be cut back, using clippers to cut each branch just above the leaf node, leaving only two or three leaves behind. Koki has no patience for this and so simply whacks away at the bushes with his machete. This means that there are inevitable branch stumps visible on the shrubbery for as long as it takes for the new growth to hide them. I don't like to see these branch stumps. Koki, I am convinced, knows that they'll be hidden eventually, so who cares? A matter of his patience beating out my esthetics.

This year I tried again; I even took the clippers and demonstrated on a branch or two of the yesterday-today-and-tomorrow bush (a shrub with white, lavender, and purple flowers) in the lee of the house. I then had the amazing confidence to drive off to town for some errands. Hours later I came back to find that what had been a pretty bushy bush had been almost entirely stripped of branches so that it now looked like a small tree with about six leaves flapping around on top. Worse, he had done the same with the once-magnificent magenta bougainvillea in front of the house. The subject of pruning obviously required more strategic thought.

A few days later, I explained to Koki that the new shape of the poor yesterday-today-and-tomorrow bush was not what I'd had in mind, and I made the shape of a big ball with my arms in the air. I wanted it to look like a ball, I said, not like a tree. And I repeated that I wanted him to use the clippers.

"Oh, I see what you mean," he said, as if we had not already had this conversation every year for the past ten.

"*Bueno,*" I said and went upstairs.

Later, from the kitchen window, I watched as Koki whacked away at a bush with his machete in one of the gardens on the windward side of the house. After he'd whacked a good third of it off, he pulled the clippers out of his back pocket and proceeded to remove the branch stumps.

Whatever works, I thought, smiling to myself.

92

I had never been a gardener – of any kind – until my parents moved into the vacation home I'd built for them next door. My father decided to import his bonsai. I thought this was ridiculous, given they would be here only three months at a time and he could park them at a nursery near home. It was a multi-ministry nightmare getting the necessary import permits, but they arrived at the airport, all seven denuded, soil-free, fumigated, stamped-by-the-U.S.-Department-of-Agriculture bonsai, hungry for repotting here in Costa Rica.

Three years later, half of them were dead ... and I was divorced and living with Roger.

The gardener had watered them to death; so, before returning to the States, Dad brought his last sad *ficus benjamina* for me to tend while he was gone. It was a peace offering. During that long and ugly divorce, both my ex-husband and my father had behaved so badly that I stopped speaking to my father for a year. He had sided with my ex, refused to help me financially and told me to go back to the States and get a job. I was almost fifty, and I was forced to ask myself why I had remained in a marriage with such an abuser for so many years.

The revelation: I had been trained for it. That's when murder entered my heart – and I saw the moment as a spiritual crisis. I sought help.

A year after the divorce was final, it took as much emotional exhaustion as courage finally to tell Dad why I had been so angry. But even though he didn't fully understand how I had felt abused, he apologized, and we both tried harder after that, although the tension was ever palpable.

One of the ways he made me feel bad when I was growing up was by calling me irresponsible. Hence, turning over his bonsai to me was a statement that – at least for the moment – I was trustworthy. Of course, I jumped at it, just like the hungry puppy I'd always been.

Taking this for the gift that it was, I determined I wouldn't kill his bonsai – but I was in no way prepared for what it required. I found a slice of log leaning against the bodega. The wood had curved inward as it dried, making a long, rustic tray. I laid it over a couple of cinder blocks under the grapefruit tree and arranged the three *ficus* on top.

How to deal with the scratchy black stuff on the edges of the leaves? Fungus or insect? The books my father had left all dealt with North American pests, and the instructions on the pesticide label were for *acres* of Costa Rican crops. On the phone, Dad and I agreed to try leaf pruning instead. For someone used to whacking back tropical vegetation with a machete, this was not my kind of pruning! I carried a small rattan stool out under the grapefruit tree and sat down with the Japanese pruning shears, and the first thing I discovered was that I had to learn to see each individual leaf. Each one had to be carefully snipped so as not to damage potential shoots developing underneath. The open-handled Japanese shears felt good in the hand, the metal warm, their shape perfect. It took about two hours. When I was finished, my eyes were sore and my back ached. Hard work, bonsai.

The next day a few more leaves had to go. And then suddenly I started to see the trees themselves: the structure of the branches, the stumps left behind from bad limb-pruning. I took the curved trimmers – another wonderful Japanese tool – and attacked the stumps. It was like performing surgery; I wanted the bark to heal cleanly.

As I worked, turning each tree, I began to see the parts: the crown, the front, the curves, the balance of branches, awkward limbs, twigs crossing at ugly angles. The trees were in terrible shape.

"How are the bonsai?" my father asked the next time he called.

"A little better, I think." I wasn't sure exactly what to report.

"Are you enjoying it?" he asked.

I wasn't sure what to say to this, either.

Each day there were fewer and fewer leaves to remove, and I began to notice some new shoots coming. It took an act of courage to pinch my first shoot. Dad had been so worried about the trees' survival, he hadn't wanted me to remove any shoots at all. But I was developing confidence. Before each pinch I had to think: if this shoot keeps growing in this direction and becomes a branch, it will cross that branch at a bad angle, or it will throw the tree off balance. Or, if I pinch here, it might force the tree (the living tree!) to push out growth in another direction. As I snipped and pinched and trimmed, each cut would weep a sticky, white bloody sap. I had read that this blood was necessary to protect the wound from the elements and to bring specialized cells to grow new bark over the injury.

Dylan Thomas's line, "The force that through the green fuse drives the flower," trailed through my head like a mantra.

Every day there were more shoots, some unfolding into bright, shiny leaves with other tiny shoots nudging their way behind them. Even on the sickest tree: first one shoot, then three, then nine. I started to look more closely at the bark and recognize the difference between skin living and dead, and I learned that, as long as there was a living green fuse inside the trunk, any part of the tree could flower again.

My father was really pleased, the next time we talked, that the worst tree was showing signs of recovery.

There were insects on the trees – spiders and a daddy longlegs. Something told me to leave them alone. This is part of Nature too, I thought. Trees in the wild are host to a million creatures, many of which help them. Perhaps the spiders would eat other insects that weren't good for the trees. One day I found a spider's nest, four leaves drawn together with silk into a cocoon to hide the eggs from the birds. Daily I watched this nest. Which of the spiders made it? Was one of them keeping her eye on it as I was? There was another creature – with an exquisite black and white carapace – that skittered sideways like a tiny crab. I found a gecko living under one of the pots. He sat perfectly still, eyeing me, as I sat perfectly still, eyeing him.

Then I noticed that the bark on the sickest tree looked bubbly. I ran to the books and identified scale. Each book had something different to suggest, and one was opposed to the use of chemicals at all. In a panic, I mixed up a solution of dishwashing soap and water and, after picking each individual insect off the bark with a pair of tweezers, I sprayed the trunk with the soap to kill any remaining eggs. I hated to report this disaster to my father, especially since it was obvious the scale had been there for a while and I just hadn't known enough to see it. Its color was so close to that of the bark and the "bubbles" so tiny that my father would have had to use a magnifying glass to find them. I think this depressed him.

My enthusiasm and confidence dimmed as, day after day, I struggled to find and remove the scale, and I imagined a new note of disapproval in my father's voice as we talked about the problem.

One day the farrier came over to shoe my mare and tied her to the grapefruit tree, as usual. Suddenly I heard her shriek – horses spook so easily – and I rushed outside to find all three bonsai upended on the ground and in instant need of repotting. Back to the books and all their intimidating information about root pruning and soil mixtures. All I had available was black earth rich with the minerals that have been pumping for millennia out of the volcano.

My friend Francisco always quoted a Chinese proverb: "If a problem has a solution, there's no need worrying about it ... and if it *doesn't* have a solution, there's no need worrying about it." I took several deep breaths and cleared part of Roger's long workbench to make room for the job. The roots were in bad shape: long taproots had thickened and curled around the insides of the pots, and the feeder roots were poorly developed. Cutting away the taproots would leave very little in the way of a root system at all, but it had to be done. With more patience than I've ever exercised in my life, I washed and pruned and combed out the roots before setting the trees back into their pots with our local dirt mixed with a little sand for drainage. I was keenly aware that what I was doing could kill the trees; they were just barely recovering from the stress of the scale, and now I was stressing them big time.

After brushing the new soil around them and carefully adding water so as not to disturb the arrangements, I finally stepped back and looked at the new bonsai, beginning to feel a little pleased with myself.

The rains came. Driving, torrential tropical rains sweeping the length of Lake Arenal, gathering force that threatened to swamp the *ficus* out of their pots. I cleared a tiny area under the shed against the bodega wall. Roger was building cabinets, and the shed was littered with lumber, tools, and sawdust, but it was my only choice. Every morning the leaves were covered with sawdust. Every morning I would spritz them clean. When the bad weather settles in around the lake, the sun disappears. The *ficus* got waterlogged. On rare sunny days I took them out into the yard to get a blast of light and warmth to dry them out. It was a holding action, a five-month siege, during the middle of which my parents came back.

Gratefully, I carried the bonsai over to their house and set them up on the verandah out of the weather. Inside, I tore all the sheets off the furniture, lighted the water heater and the stove, made fresh ice. When I brought them home from the airport, Dad was disconcerted to find the bonsai on his verandah.

"I thought you'd want them back," I said.

He grunted.

I figured he was tired from the trip and I went home. The next day he drove over with the bonsai. "I don't really want them anymore," he said.

I was crushed. All that work and panic and heartache to save his trees!

"I'm glad you've gotten interested in them," he went on. "You keep them."

Once again my anger at him threatened to swamp me, and I felt tears burning. Not a word of thanks! But I turned away to lift a pot out of the trunk of his car to carry it back to the rustic shelf still straddling the cinder blocks under the shed.

I lived with my anguish for a couple of days before I got up the nerve to speak to him. "I've been thinking," I said finally, as we drove into town for some errands, "that you didn't want the bonsai back because they don't look as good as they did before."

"That's partly it," he admitted. "When I first bought them, they were so full and green. But it's also true that I've lost interest."

I read that to mean that he was afraid he couldn't care for them anymore, but there was nothing I could say. He was 78 years old with cataracts and a bad neck. And he would always lack the grace to express appreciation for what I had done.

My reward was to be the trees themselves. For Christmas he gave me $50 to go to a nursery in San José and buy an addition to my "collection."

Now the labor was all mine and I could start to love the bonsai for themselves, and not because I was trying to please my difficult father. The shift was noticeable. No more panic. A lot more patience. More courage in my design decisions. I could let the trees bring me into their peace.

I started to see big trees differently: those bent by the Trade Winds, all their branches reaching in the same direction; those clinging precariously to eroded banks, half their roots exposed; those sporting dead branches, perching places for sharp-eyed hawks; those with lightning-scarred and twisted trunks; and those with bleached and rotted boles for the squirrels.

I hunted down a small nursery in the dust bowl of the lowlands, where the proprietor wandered among his few specimens barefoot. My total investment in four wretched little trees in nursery plastic was about $4. But I brought them home, root-pruned and repotted them with all the patience and love that a Zen monk would lavish on a 200-year-old pine. My collection was growing.

Sometime later I met a bonsai artist who told me that an important quality of a bonsai is its history: whether physically old or not, where it comes from, who gave it to you – the emotional content – has value for the Japanese. He told me that Zen monks see a tree as a ladder between earth and heaven, by which man can ascend to God and God can descend to man. He also told me there are no female bonsai masters.

Six weeks before their scheduled departure for the States, my mother broke her hip. The four-hour ambulance ride over the mountains to San José was agonizingly painful, and when they got back, Dad drove over to announce that they were giving up on Costa Rica; they needed to live in a place where good medical care was more accessible. The decision was understandable, if painful, especially since they had just been talking about making Costa Rica their permanent home. Mom loved it here.

It was impossible, then, for me to accept their leaving without feeling it as a rejection, too, of me. Just as it was impossible for my father even to try to make me feel otherwise.

Taking care of the bonsai has been good training. My eyes don't tire anymore. I can shift my focus from close in (the new shoots) to mid-range (the health of the leaves) to miniaturized long-distance (the overall shape). Back and forth. Seeing, understanding what the tree needs, discovering how it heals itself.

Taking care of my father's bonsai has deepened my understanding of another living thing. To say that it is a miracle – this life form with its green fuse and white blood, its unfurling leaves, its innate thrusting out from the center – has been said before. But the bigger miracle here is me: the observer, the tender, the servant of these trees, the new lover of growing things, the one who is also growing.

My parents are both gone now. But my father's three *ficus benjamina* have survived many years of my intermittent care. When bonsais have been around this long, one has to think seriously of whom to leave them to. Roger's solution is simply to plant them in the ground. A number of my bonsai failures are now robust trees around the little house. But none of those ever had a *history*.

I think I will try to engage Koki in this bonsai work. After running the weed-whacker all over the farm in areas that were not in serious need of cutting, even he realized that he was running out of work because of the drier conditions, and he admitted as much.

"Any special chores?" he asked me the other day.

My mother was a gardener of flowers. She must have planted 500 daffodils around the spacious backyard of one house we lived in. She was "house proud" and wanted everything outside to be as beautiful as it was in. At another house, to keep the lawn free of crabgrass, she, my little sister and I would crawl around in the damp yard in the late summer afternoons when the angle of the sun revealed the reddish stems. We pulled them out one-by-one. In Florida she joined the condominium garden committee and almost single-handedly redid the landscaping around the low buildings. In one raised bed in front of her door she planted a plaster cherub. She brought this to Costa Rica and perched it, along with every other flowering shrub Rafa could bring her, above the retaining wall behind the house. I still keep this creature, although Rosa accidentally knocked its feet off with her mop. My taste doesn't run to plaster cherubim, but this is one of the small ways I honor my mother's memory, and it reminds me that she gave me more than I was aware of at the time.

Two days in a row I've been able to do yoga out on the verandah, and this morning I heard a "new" bird – that is, one I hadn't noticed before. It was so loud I was convinced it was on a rafter right over my head. It had a beautiful song, full of trills and warbles. I broke off my yoga to see if I could spot it – it had to be nearby. In vain I scanned the rafters, the eaves, the rail, the nearby tree branches, while it tantalized me with new bursts of song. Finally, I looked over at the hammock in the corner, just as it sounded off again. A tiny house wren, not four inches long from tail to beak-tip, dull brown, nothing special about it at all, except it clung bravely to one of the hammock ropes swinging in the wind singing its heart out.

On Valentine's Day ("Friendship Day" in Costa Rica) it seems that the "drier season" is really here, with stunning, cloudless days that invite one out of doors. Yesterday I went swimming in the pool at the nearby hotel. The water was *freezing,* but I did a few laps to warm up, and then just lolled and paddled in the water feeling the sun on my face and arms and watching a vulture laze around above in the pool of heaven.

It's dry enough that I took a watering can out to the seedlings we've parked in the shade of the *corteza* tree to await transplanting in May when they'll be stronger. I noticed that Koki hasn't been paying any attention to these, and the plastic bags are full of weeds. As I watered, my eyes on the slender stems, I saw something *else* growing in one of the bigger bags. I followed it with my eyes up and around the trunk of the old *corteza* until it terminated in a pair of strangler fig leaves. What an opportunistic parasite! It feels like *The Invasion of the Body Snatchers*. I'm not going to let this one get away with it; the *corteza* is just too precious to me. When Koki comes tomorrow morning, I'll have him move all those seedlings and rip out the strangler, roots and all.

Around the back of the house, I hauled out the hose and gave the pineapple patch a watering too. We have one now almost ready for harvest – much bigger than previous ones – and another flower is just emerging. I guess that California red worm compost Evelio's been cooking up in the woodshed has helped the pineapples along. I'll try to remember to give them another boost when the serious rains start up again.

The only moisture we've had recently is the misty *llovizna*, which drifts daily across the lake in late afternoon when the westering sun paints a perfect rainbow between us and the far shore, every color sharply defined, the 180-degree arc seemingly anchored – tantalizingly – just on the other side of Evelio's garden. Rainbows are not unusual around here, but every one stops the heart for just a second, reminding me that where we live is a treasure indeed. And, since a rainbow is nothing more than a phenomenon of light and moisture as seen from a particular angle, it occurs to me that there is always a rainbow *somewhere*.

This afternoon I showed Koki the strangler going after the *corteza amarillo*. And then, since I had spotted a few more blooms on that tree, I reminded him that we wanted to watch carefully for seeds again this year. *This* is when he finally told me that it's almost impossible to grow *corteza* from seed (if you can even *find* the seeds), and that – tapping his finger to his forehead in that universal gesture of arcane knowledge – an "old man in the country" had told him that the best way to propagate this tree is from cuttings, buried horizontally in the ground. Even though Koki has known for over a year that Roberta of the La Reserva Forest Foundation has been desperate to get her hands on some *cortezas* for their nursery, only now is he doling these details out to me.

He had just finished carting away all the wood he'd chopped up from the wind damage, and he said we had lots of "cuttings" of an appropriate size to plant. We selected a planting area for a few of them near the house, where it will be easy to water them during the dry season, and I asked him to set aside the rest for La Reserva. Excited by the possibility of getting more *cortezas* growing, I went right into the house to call Roberta.

While I am on the phone, Koki appears at my office door with a fair-sized log with five baby *cortezas* growing out of it, the biggest already about a foot tall. I hang up and try not to look dumbfounded. Then I remember that we'd done some cutting back of the *corteza* over a year ago, pruning the heavier branches to relieve the strain on the main trunk in the wind. This log had obviously come from that earlier pruning, and the seedlings were thriving. Some "old man in the country" told him about this? Or did Koki just discover it on the woodpile himself and decide to let me know?

Koki is a natural with dogs, and he has always adopted one of our pets as his companion on his daily rounds. Fortuna is his current favorite, and Flor always tags along. Miraculously, all our dogs have both adored and obeyed him, seemingly without his needing to say or do anything obvious. This morning I needed to talk to him about where to plant the Christmas poinsettias, and as soon as I got outside, both Fortuna and Flor were all over my new shirt. I have yelled "Down!" at them a thousand times, always using the same forceful downward motion of my palms, but to no avail. It's reached the point where I don't even *like* these two dogs anymore. I didn't invite them into my life; they just arrived, full-fledged, and full of bad habits.

When it didn't work again this morning, Koki pointed his finger at Fortuna and went "Shhhh!" and they both moved away from me with alacrity. I have heard him do this "Shhhh!" before, and recently I've been trying to imitate it. But it doesn't work when I do it.

I begged him: "Koki, what is the secret to getting these dogs to behave?" He smiled and said I just had to show them who was boss. I thought I *had* been showing them who was boss, with my forceful gestures and strong words, but I haven't yet – as my biologist friend Susanna suggested – bitten Fortuna's lip. I've done nothing, it seems, except to get desperately frustrated. So Koki said, "You have to show them affection *(cariño)*." I said, "I do," reaching down to pat two perfectly docile pets. "But *then*," he went on, "you have to show them who rules." With that he lunged toward Fortuna, right knee bent, right arm extended, as in the fencing maneuver, and said in a commanding voice (like God speaking to Charlton Heston from the burning bush),

"Hablé!" I have spoken.

Of course. I have been speaking to the dogs in *English*.

Koki has taken two days off to harvest the non-organic beans he has planted on a small plot provided by a big landholder near his village. I applaud this farmer for lending out part of his property this way, but I know that the same little plots will yield fewer and fewer beans over time. Koki doesn't know this yet and so makes fun (not to his face) of Evelio for his efforts at organic gardening, and he has so far refused to be of any help unless I specifically ask him to, as with the Fortuna fence. The other day, he came up to my office with the special information that Evelio had better get about the harvesting of his beans, or they would rot.

Evelio hasn't been around much lately, but when he called to ask Roger's help for a Swiss boy who had broken his ankle windsurfing, I mentioned what Koki had said about his beans. He assured me that it was just the wind drying them out, and that they had time yet. I notice that today Evelio is here with a visiting Mexican windsurfer to start getting those beans in – good harvest or no.

And the second day that Koki was supposed to be absent harvesting his beans, he came here instead.

"What happened?" I asked him.

"Everything was rotted," he said. "A total loss."

The combination of the wet December and the high winds has taken its toll on everyone, it seems, organic or not. I have to remember that this is not just the loss of a small crop – something that can be made up in a future planting, say – but the loss of beans on the table of a family of six for a year. Now they will have to be bought at store prices, which are stabilizing for now, but the world economic crisis still has surprises in store for us all, and these will affect the poor of the planet first.

Inclining his head toward Evelio's garden, Koki wanted to know what I wished him to do with that piece of land after Evelio is finished with it. "You know Evelio doesn't want to plant anything else there," he said.

I nodded. "Evelio seems very discouraged. If he would just plant small plots of vegetables, instead of trying for a big cash crop like this ... " I shrugged. "I really enjoyed eating his green beans!"

"Of course, in dry season he would have to water," Koki reminded me.

And then I said it: "Well, if it were just a *small* garden, I'd be willing." So shut my mouth. If nothing else, my daily writing of this *book* depends on it.

Then Koki said his father-in-law was growing lettuce, and that the plants were *this* high (he held his hand out flat at knee-level). "I can bring you some, if you want." I said that would be very nice. "They're grown with fertilizer and everything," he said.

No sooner had I written that the "drier" season had arrived than another norther blew through, with winds strong enough to make it difficult to close the car door, if you were parked in the wrong direction. It has happened that the unguarded have actually *lost* car doors in Tilarán. Always better to park the car – like a yacht – nose to the wind.

I feared unnecessarily for the *corteza amarillo*. It is now bursting into bloom, the exoskeleton still alive, yellow explosions of color all over the remaining branches. I inwardly give thanks for another year of life for this glorious old tree. From now on, the season *burgeons*.

Through the branches and flowers of the *corteza* I can see the lacy, pale green flowers of the avocado tree. The hundreds of trees in the reforestation areas, most of whose names I don't know, are flowering in bright reds, pinks, and whites. And the *oropéndolas* are beginning their evening gathering in the compound tree down by the runoff creek. Every afternoon at about four o'clock, they start to move, heralding their easterly trek with little *cheeps* so unlike their usually liquid voices, as hundreds cross the *quebrada* just over our heads, heading for their roost. It's an impressive sight, and their cries stop all conversation.

I have been dedicating my days to the plants on the verandah, including my many neglected so-called bonsai. Humbly, I like to remember that the Japanese word means nothing more than *tree-in-a-pot*, because I hesitate to call these poor examples anything other than disasters. So: pruning; pulling weeds (including the ever-invasive ferns); spraying for scale, aphids, spider mites, or anything else that's eating at them (I am no organic *bonsaista*); shuffling them around into sunnier or shadier locations, depending on their various maladies. The problem for me now is that the arthritis in my fingers makes all the work of repotting and cutting and moving a major exercise, so I postpone it until they're half-dead.

This time I'm seriously motivated, since my sister and her husband are coming for a visit, and he also has an interest in bonsai. I'd be ashamed for them to see my poor specimens in their current state. They both have gardening genes – my sister Alison directly from our mother, and Dick from his father. When they married in Dick's small town in the northeastern Dutch province of Groningen, I flew to the Netherlands for their June wedding. The front yard of his family's row house was a riot of color: there were tulips – obviously – but also every other kind of flower, and all jammed together so tightly that there was no room to walk except on the rigid little path from the sidewalk to the front door. The backyard was the same, but there was a narrow porch with a huge birdcage that had a couple of what I thought of then as exotic tropical birds in it.

I like to think of Dick's journey to bonsai – from his father's gardens to the U.S. with his new bride, then to the Northwest with its strong Asian influences – as a less complicated trip than mine was. Either way, it's a pleasure to be able to share our love of bonsai with each other.

The potted black begonia on the verandah is blooming. Its leaves feel like velvet, of a green so dark it is almost black, with red undersides and fleshy, red-spotted stems. The blooms, at the ends of half-yard-long, almost translucent spears, emerge as fist-sized clusters of unspectacular, rosy, bivalve bracts that open to reveal minuscule yellow flowers. The whole plant, with a diameter of over two feet, seen from a distance, with its velvety black leaves and fleshy pink-tipped shoots sticking out all over, looks like something from another planet. I am finding that this sense of strangeness occurs with greater and greater frequency the more closely I observe a thing in Nature. The complexity, the variety, the sheer mechanics of how a thing is put together, the parts, the whole, the synchronicity with the other creatures around it, all astonish and amaze, as if I were a visitor exploring for the first time an alien sphere.

And more amazing still is that, for everything observed in this small world of mine, there are so many others yet unseen.

One of my chores on the verandah has been to cut back the basil. I have seven pots of it out there, all gone leggy and struggling with aphids. Evelio's organic insecticide is the most potent thing I've ever used on these aphids, but they need to be sprayed directly in order to be killed, and when there's a lot of foliage, some get missed. A drastic cutting-back was the only solution. The infected branches I simply tossed over the rail, but the healthy ones were starting to accumulate in my basket in a quantity sufficient to make Rosa pause in her mopping of the deck to ask me whether I made pesto with macadamia or pine nuts.

Until that moment, it hadn't occurred to me to make pesto. I hadn't thought at all what to do with all this basil, but pesto sounded like a good idea. I had both macadamia and pine nuts in the house (the macadamias are local, the pine nuts a treasure brought by my friend Shirley from a small town 400 miles north of Toronto), plenty of garlic and extra virgin olive oil, even real Parmesan cheese imported from Parma. I hadn't made pesto in years, since jars of it often make their way into the Tilarán supermarkets and washing and pulling off all those leaves from the stems is a chore.

Italian pesto isn't a staple of the Costa Rican diet, but Rosa worked for many tourist seasons at an Italian restaurant near here. So when I had it all made up, I invited her to sample it.

"Better," she said. "At the restaurant they don't use any cheese. And why would theirs be runnier? Too much oil? Why wouldn't they use cheese – because it's cheaper?"

I confessed that, yes, no cheese certainly made their pesto cheaper. I pulled out a jar of the commercial stuff and read the list of ingredients; no cheese there either. I dipped my spoon into the lovely pale green paste I had just made, closed my eyes, and ... ah, so densely green and nutty, with just enough cheesy sharpness to make all the difference.

Koki informed me that the cattleman renting the next-door property has been fixing the fence.

"Finally!" I said, much relieved.

"No, no, it's a *cochinada*, a real mess," he said.

Koki has been watching the man and his sons propping up the rotted posts with shims – branches cut from the trees – and re-stapling the wire where it had come loose. Now I'm in a true Costa Rican pickle. If, as Koki assures me, the cattleman's lease requires him to maintain the fence, then, under the law, it is *him* I have to sue. But he seems like a nice enough guy; he's *trying* to be a good neighbor in spite of what are obviously limited resources, and I don't want to create problems for him. Creating problems for the *owner* of the property, on the other hand, would be a delight, but I can't get to her as long as this man is leasing her land.

So once again we wait. We wait for the cattleman's lease to be up. We wait for him to move out. We wait for his flimsily repaired fence to fall. But most of all we wait for the cows. They will surely come.

March
Finally ... Beans!

We have eaten some of Evelio's beans! His mood has been so dismal for so long that I was sure the entire harvest was lost, just as Koki's was. But, no, he and his new Mexican friend, Guillermo, have been out there harvesting, and they put about three cups in a little bag for me. I asked Evelio how to cook *tiernos,* un-dried beans, since I've only cooked dried before, and those in the pressure-cooker. I didn't want to over-cook these pretty red ones. Evelio's recipe was nothing more than to put them in a regular pot with water and cook until done, so I had to experiment, which meant watching them for half an hour or so. I used far too much water, so I've saved the cooking liquid in a jar to add it to a soup. The beans came out fine; although neither of us is crazy about beans, it was good to be eating something home-grown in Evelio's garden at last.

The day of the harvest, Evelio pointed to the plants off in the corner of his bean field, where the old orchard meets the property line. There's less wind in that corner, he informed me, so the plants there are producing well. I will forgive him for failing to remember that a few months ago I suggested that same spot as a good place to plant vegetables. But that's what he intends to do, and I send up a silent prayer of thanks for Guillermo, who has revived Evelio's excitement for his organic garden.

With Roger off in San José comes a crisis with the roof of the little house.

While Koki and I are chatting at my office door about what's needed to fix it, I see a bug crawling up the arm of his rain jacket. He plucks it off and holds it out for me to see: a rhinoceros beetle, or *cornizuelo*. I have seen impressive examples of these in dead bug collections, but it's the first time I've seen one here: a shiny dark brown, with a sharply upward-curved frontal horn, about two-and-a-half inches long from end to end. Not a pretty thing to look at, but remarkable. I went to the only source we have on insects, the encyclopedic *Costa Rican Natural History*, to find out more about it.

What makes this bug especially interesting to me is that it lays its eggs in very large, old logs, the size of the log necessary to the long gestation period—three-to-four years. In the tropics, wood on the forest floor rots quickly, so only the biggest fallen trees can be used for incubation, and it's just these trees that are disappearing from the tropics. Deforestation is making the rhinoceros beetle scarcer. We've lost a few big, old trees around here to wind, floods and lightning over the years, and, if they fall in the yard, Koki cuts them up and stacks the wood for future use. The wood at the bottom of these stacks rots, of course, but there's still plenty left for firewood, and now I can appreciate that the big logs at the bottom have created a habitat for the *cornizuelos*. More forest, more logs, more bugs, more of *all* the interdependent creatures of the amazing ecosystem that is the tropics.

Until I found heliconias growing wild on our property, I wasn't much interested in them. That is, I assumed that –

like orchids – they'd require special conditions or, worse, special care, so I ignored them. Heliconias, such as the bird of paradise, are quintessential tropical flowers. Stood up in great hotel lobby arrangements, they don't even look real. Which is why, when I saw some brightly painted wooden ones at the home center in Liberia, I bought them, and put them in a tallish clay pot on the stoop of the garage entrance into the house to brighten it up a bit. Within two days, Fortuna had chewed them to splinters.

So imagine my delight, returning from the gate with the newspaper one morning, when I chanced to look to my right just past the big compound tree and saw a whole clutch of *Heliconia latispatha* blooming at the edge of the reforestation ground – multiple blood-red, boat-shaped bracts sticking out from a zigzag yellow stem, just as showy as any cultivar in a flower shop. I was also chagrined. Why wasn't this wonderful bed of heliconias growing up by the house? Surely Koki knew it was there – he knows every *inch* of this property. I hurriedly instructed him to transplant some of them to a wind-protected area in the shade of the *quebrada* where I could see them from the verandah outside my office. And, for two weeks while the ones at the edge of the forest bloomed, Rosa clipped them and put them in the large glass vase on the table inside the front door where people would see them.

Encouraged, I picked up a few others at Tere's nursery, including a pendant variety, *Heliconia pogonantha*. This one is truly bizarre-looking, the tall yellow stem of the mature plant curling over into a six-foot series of upside-down red bracts bursting in a loose spiral out of the center. And this is the one that has just started to bloom, a bit of gorgeous brilliance in my otherwise soggy, gray-green garden.

Like bromeliads, heliconias are whole ecosystems unto themselves and are especially attractive to several hummingbirds, with which they have co-evolved. The hollow bracts contain a liquid that is home to protozoa and insect larvae. The undersides of the broad leaves make perfect nesting sites for hummers and white bats. Butterflies lay eggs in the foliage, which later serves as food for their caterpillars. The tiny blue fruits attract the blue-crowned manakins, fly-catchers and motmots, among many others. And, in one book about snakes in Costa Rica I saw a photograph of a jewel-like golden eyelash viper coiled around a yellow heliconia waiting to catch a hummingbird – a case of perfect and deadly camouflage.

At this time of year, the full moon sets right outside our western bedroom window, as big and shiny as a new car. Here, where there's no air pollution, even a quarter-moon lights up the landscape, and a full moon you can almost read by. When it sinks behind the *uruca* tree outside our window and the wind blows the branches to and fro, the moon flashes on and off like the signal light on a battleship. Sleep is impossible. Not only because of the light, but because the cats get restless and think it's time for one of us to get up and feed them.

Ever since we moved into this house, I have been puzzling over what to do about curtains or blinds or shades for the windows. I don't favor formal window arrangements. Bamboo shades are more my style, but they're not really private. I even bought 23 yards of material to make Roman shades, but the stuff turned out to be *not* washable, so it still hangs in a plastic bag in the guestroom closet. Because we're on the second floor and backed up to a forest, it would be impossible to see in unless someone were standing on the verandah outside our bedroom or using a mighty telescope from the other side of the lake; and so I've left the windows uncovered. This means a bad night or two while the full moon sets in a certain part of the sky.

But the mornings! Ah, waking up in the morning in the middle of the tree canopy on one side of the bedroom and with a long view of the pearly lake at dawn on the other makes a bad night or two well worth it.

Until I came to Costa Rica in 1988, I had never traveled outside the U.S. on my own. Alone I had traveled on business all over the country when there was a corporate travel agent to handle the details and before the airlines were deregulated. With a mini-version of the Official Airline Guide in your briefcase, you could walk up to any airline counter – as if it were a bus station – and swap whatever ticket you held for the next flight out.

To arrange a trip to Costa Rica, something my former husband promoted my doing (at least *his* certainty of future happiness in any Central American country magically assured), I had to make all the arrangements myself with the help of the only existing travel guide written more than a decade before. We were going to be in a Tampa resort for a business conference, an easy jumping-off point for me while he returned home. I clutched my ticket, my very rough itinerary, and a Berlitz Spanish audio tape in my fist, as we parted at the edge of the alligator-ridden golf course.

His logic had been that if I could travel comfortably to Costa Rica alone, we could live there! The alcoholic fantasies I bought into ...

But, since I too was looking for an escape from the multiple stresses I had been living under, I dared to go. After all, it was totally credible. Hadn't we lunched at his private club with another member, whose wife was an Honorary Consul, and who had explained to us the ease with which one could get residency there? My former husband was proud of his membership in the club, and proud that his wife and business partner could do a reconnaissance without him. "The press of business," et cetera, kept him home while I flew off to San José.

I had a week and a rental car. The agent took twenty minutes to walk around the vehicle to identify its many faults, which he noted on a paper I had to sign before he consigned the car to my care. The trunk didn't open, the right window didn't roll down, the driver's side door had to be opened from the outside, there was no air-conditioning, and the dings and dents were multiple. The only hotel of which I had been able to assure myself was the old Hotel Amstel, just south of the pretty Parque Morazán. It was the dingiest little room I had ever seen; the walls were brown, and what came out of the shower was intermittent and not always warm. I give credit to the restaurant staff, however; they were always courteous and ready to help me with whatever I didn't understand on the menu.

A woman alone in a country where, at that time, I was a rarity, was always greeted with surprise. "Do you have children?" was the inevitable first question everywhere I went, the supposition being that, if I had them, what the hell was I doing wandering around the planet by myself? In response to this question, with my limited Spanish, I would always clutch my abdomen with both hands and say, "I can't." This always elicited a tut-tut of sympathy and an improvement of *confianza* in any brief encounter.

In central San José I went to a bookstore in search of a map. The only one available was topographical, but at least it indicated the major roads, which, on the ground, were not signed. So, from the relative security of the city I made my way south as far as the Tapantí Nature Reserve, where I was the only visitor to the remote banks of the Río Reventazón and a magical, 330-foot jungle waterfall. At the musty little motel on the banks of the river, the restaurant had already closed when I arrived – and that was the only restaurant in the tiny town of Orosi. Aside from one other gringo couple, I was the only guest, and they too were hungry. We decided to pool resources: I contributed two packs of cheese and peanut butter crackers, and they one mango and two bananas. In the morning after a huge *tico* breakfast, I visited the unadorned and serene seventeenth-century church – the kind of rustic, intimate chapel where I always feel more at home than in the grand cathedrals of Europe. Then I drove my rattley vehicle halfway across the country to Monteverde in the north, up a hot, dusty road that almost choked both me and the little car.

Covered with dust as I stood at the desk of my hotel, I asked for a beer to take to my room, where I showered, beer in hand, for a full half-hour. There were almost no tourists, but there was a guided horseback tour that I saw posted the next morning at breakfast. It was April, quetzal-mating time. I hadn't known anything about these elusive birds, but indeed the guide led me to a breeding male in the canopy high overhead, his long iridescent green tail feathers and red breast shockingly brilliant in the gloom of the cloud forest.

Why would I move to such a country? I had my own fantasy: a lake, a small fishing boat, a modest adobe tile-roofed house – and my grand piano.

Finally: a carrot, a head of lettuce, a miniature green chile! Unbelievably, the weeds that are overgrowing the bean field are protecting some of the vegetables from the wind. Roger had told me that Evelio is considering growing organic vegetables over at the hotel down the road where I swim. There's a plot over there behind a windbreak. This makes me anxious. For all that Evelio makes me crazy, I don't want to lose him – I've already decided on the title for this book! So, when he showed up this morning pushing his load of horse manure for the worms, I leaned over the rail to try to talk him into staying here. I told him I'd heard that organic farmer Leo's been selling a hundred thousand *colones'* worth of worm compost a month. I suggested he plant his *frijol tapado* in the area we had explored and told him he could go ahead and plant vegetables among the tree seedlings in the reforestation lot on the other side of the *quebrada*. I am desperate for him to stay, and even tell him that it hurts me to think of his leaving.

In the Northern Zone the harvest is down by 50 percent because of the ugly weather. As a consequence, Evelio's beans are worth more now than he'd projected they would be. He told me this morning, holding a sad-looking bean plant with only eleven pods on it, about a few acres he had planted with his brothers years ago. The plants were so high (indicating with his palm), so bushy, and they had three times as many pods on them. The harvest was in the tons. They had to load the huge sacks onto the backs of horses to carry them away. But, because everybody was growing beans that year, there was no market for their crop. They had to dry them and stow them and eat what they could themselves, giving the rest away. *Now* he's beginning to appreciate that the law of supply and demand may be working in his favor. And I think his little offerings – the carrot, the head of lettuce and the miniature chile – are a way of thanking me for my persistence, and maybe even my patience.

Mid-March. The first sunny day that didn't have a chilly edge to it. We have never been more aware that we're in the northern hemisphere than we have this winter, as the eastern U.S. has been blasted with weather systems that have pushed front after front of cold air and moisture south. Snow in Florida, anyone? Today Rosa threw open all the windows and doors to air the place out, and she scrubbed and brushed and mopped and dusted with fervor. It finally feels like a new year!

Watering the pineapple plot this afternoon for the first time in over a week, I discovered a huge fire-ants' nest where the edible ginger should be. I turned the hose nozzle on "stream" and blasted them out of there. The damn things nest everywhere. The ornamental beds are so overgrown that you don't spot them until they're releasing their furious venom all over your feet. You screech, jump back, whip off your sandals, brush off your feet, and then whack the sandals on the ground a few times to shake off any excess ants. Out in the lawn, the nests are easier to see and avoid: just dark little hills of black earth popping up in the middle of nowhere. Roberta told me that human urine kills off these nests. Not wanting to use nasty chemicals on the Reserve, they've experimented with other substances. I told this to Koki, and he laughed. Obviously, I haven't seen him trying it.

Suddenly begins the tantalizing symphony of birdsong. Three sun-filled days and, from the newly washed hammock, I gaze at the luminescent sky at sunset and see the manakins zipping around in the bare branches of the *guanacaste* behind the house. I think I can connect their song to their flight, but it takes much closer observation than I've been capable of to identify most birds by their song. All I could see was their small *shapes,* shadows against the gloaming, and associate their little *cheeps* with their forms.

There are others now, new spring sounds (since I am

newly listening) that frustrate me because of my ignorance. Some I have *seen* sing. That's the only way I can know for sure, since the books all insist on a *sighting* as a prerequisite for identification. Although once I did identify a bird (the northern jacana) whose remains – a single gray-edged yellow feather and a pair of greenish yellow feet – had been thoughtfully deposited on the front porch by one of the cats. I still have the feather. I disposed of the feet.

In the heart of every human being there is a blower of dandelions. When I was a child, no one bothered to tell me I was dispersing seeds with every wish-filled puff, but I know now that many plants create airy feathers to carry their seeds away on the breeze, from the humble dandelion to the mighty *ceiba*. I have no idea what kind of seed it was that landed on our porch this afternoon with a feathery top four inches across. I saw it while I was watering the potted plants and picked it up and marveled at its silky beauty. "Plant me," it said. I think I will.

Evelio's on his knees out there beating on his beans with a stick. He has anchored a large sheet of plastic in the middle of the bean field, on one side of which is a mound of dried bean pods. One batch at a time, he pulls them toward himself with the stick and begins to whack them, forcing them to open and release their beans. Still using the stick, he gracefully tosses the empty pods up and to one side, while to the other he slides the freed beans, where they are spread out gleaming red in the late-afternoon sun. I know that in at least one of the many images of pre-

Columbian Mesoamerican life I have seen – on a clay pot, on a temple wall – exactly this, the upward motion of the arm with the stick, the position of the head and body just so, on its knees, the same ancient rhythmic whack of the stick against the beans.

Then, from the pile of beans, Evelio gathers some into a bucket and, standing over a second sheet of plastic, he slowly pours the beans out and down, letting the wind blow away the chaff. The wind has to be just right – too much and the beans would also blow away; too little, and much of the chaff would remain. He repeats this slow pouring, this time on his knees, picking up the beans by the loving handful, slowly letting them fall into the semi-clear plastic bags I have been saving for him from the supermarket produce section. Evelio may not be getting the harvest he had hoped for, but on this breezy afternoon, out there in the sunny field, the color of the lake beyond him so blue it almost seems detached from the landscape, the volcano half-visible in the distance, Evelio seems a happy man.

Later, I go out to talk with him about his harvest. Evelio is one of those unfortunate souls who always sees the glass of milk half-empty.

"I was hoping for 300 kilos of beans, and I harvested only 30," he moaned.

"But Evelio, thirty to me sounds great for a first-year organic garden!" (Our see-saw conversations, in which he says something negative and I immediately respond with something positive, would be amusing to a gaggle of psychologists.)

He leans toward the positive this time, talking about his methods, the ancient rituals of agriculture. "This is the *campesino* way, not industrial where everything is done with tractors and seeders and harvesters. No," he says with pride, "this is the way of the *agricultor* – the *personal* way." He tells me he learned these ways as a child, first playing in the giant piles of chaff, just as we in the north played in the raked-up leaves of autumn. Then, year by year as he grew, he participated more in the work, the patient preparing of the ground, the planting, the reaping, the drying, the beating and threshing of the beans. It's in his blood. Better still, it's in his genes.

There's been another unfamiliar, very loud bird call in the *quebrada* lately, and this morning when Rosa was here it sounded off again. "What *is* that bird?" I asked her.

"It's a bird that always lived in the *quebradas* when I was growing up," she answered. "In the *campo* we call it the *pomponé*."

Thank God for The Bird Book: it includes all the local names in the index, along with their scientific and English equivalents. I was really excited when I opened the book to the color plate, because indeed I had seen this bird, the gray-necked wood rail, two of them doing their mating dance in the middle of the road that winds up the slopes of Miravalles Volcano to some hot springs there. I was with two friends, one of whom is a birder and identified them. And what a dance! – the male slowly circling the female, wings extended, red legs high-stepping, dipping his yellow beak toward his mate-to-be. We stopped the car and watched, enchanted, until a motorcycle roared by and chased the birds off. So I am not likely to forget the gray-necked wood rail and I am delighted that it's making a nest in our *quebrada*. Rosa said that the song announces that they're laying their eggs.

The blue-and-white swallows are back. They've been poking and snooping around the eaves for the last week or two, looking for a nesting site. There is at least one pair and, even though they mate throughout the year (according to The Book), they're obvious around here only in the spring, with two broods, one in March and the other in May. They're tiny, just a little over four inches long, with a white throat and belly and an almost neon-blue back and head, a smudgy charcoal gray in between. It's fun to watch their high-speed careening and swirling around the house. Over the years they have nested in the rafters under the eaves and in the ceiling of the garage, so there must something appealing or advantageous in these human locations; are they safer here from predators than they would be in the wild? The nestlings stay with their parents for a couple of months, and then we have *quantities* of swallows around the house, zooming and bombarding and tantalizing the cats, who sit as patient as sleepy-eyed sphinxes on the edge of the deck waiting for one to dart within reach. So far the pyrotechnics of the swallows have outwitted the cunning of the cats, but that doesn't keep the felines from trying. Unbelievably, Fat Frieda, the oldest and heaviest of the three, seems to have the greatest agility with birds, but she hasn't caught a swallow yet. (Roger says she *sits* on birds to kill them.)

Today I rescued one that had become confused inside the glass we've installed recently on the windward side of the verandah. I'm grateful I got to it before Frieda did. Years ago I believed I had identified the blue-and-whites on the wing, but today, cupping a tiny, frightened bird in my hands, I was assured of my swallow.

The newspaper reminds us that the equinox is here, and to be more careful in the sun because, directly overhead, its rays are more intense. Okay, not *directly*

overhead; we are ten degrees north of the equator. But from now on, the days will be lengthening ever more noticeably until the solstice three months away. Today when I was out on the sunning platform, it did indeed seem as if the sunshine were hotter, more intense. I take the digital kitchen timer with me so I don't stay out there too long; ten minutes is all I need, and I try to do it either before ten in the morning, or after three in the afternoon, when the sun's rays are more oblique. Frieda loves this sunbathing routine, and she takes advantage of my recumbent self to snuggle, rub and cuddle, and do everything possible to cover me with cat hair. Feeling the sun quite hot on my face after a while, I picked up the little timer and saw that it had stopped counting backwards at eight minutes and twenty-six seconds. I knew instantly what had happened: Frieda had sat on it.

I wanted an avenue of *robles*. It was April when I first came to Costa Rica, and the *robles de sabana* were blooming along Paseo Colón, the broad central avenue leading into San José. Many of those old *robles,* planted over a century ago, are gone now, but years ago they made a stunning colonnaded entrance to the capital. It was a happy, welcoming sight, and I was determined to copy it along the 175-yard driveway to our new house. The seedlings were only three feet tall when we planted them, and it took three years for the first of them to bloom. I had told Tere at the nursery that I wanted pink ones, just like the beautiful trees on Paseo Colón, but when the first one bloomed it was white. Last year many more bloomed, and my vision of a long, rosy colonnade was destroyed – some pinks, some whites, not at all the solid splash of color I had hoped for. This year, with some of the *robles* over ten feet tall, I'm beginning to see a different vision, a forest canopy over the gravel driveway, and in another year or two we should be almost there.

However, when I planted the *robles,* it didn't occur to me that I was planting *deciduous* trees. So many trees in Costa Rica aren't, that I just didn't think about it. This means that my forest canopy is leafless for at least a couple of months of the year. So, now you know why I am complaining that there are still plenty of ugly, insect-bitten, dried-out leaves clinging stubbornly to the *robles* and, coming up on the beginning of April and my sister's first visit since we built the house, there's not a bloom in sight, white or pink. I would be grateful for either. Meanwhile, there's a magnificent old specimen down by the bridge on the way into Tilarán that's in gorgeous rosy bloom. I have to face the fact that I'm not going to live long enough to see my *robles* look like that. But planting trees is a *future* business.

Now the days grow long. From an iridescent blue in mid-afternoon, the lake turns slowly aqua as the sun lies low and the saturated colors of the hills above the water take on a softer gray. The trees known as *lengua de vaca* (cows' tongues) between the house and the fence-line are blooming white on their wind-tortured trunks. The sky over Tenorio Volcano to the northwest now radiates pinks and mauves at sunset. Over all there is a gentler, tropical quality to the light.

I heard the first motmot this morning, a quiet, tentative wh*oop-whoop,* looking for a response. The motmots are ever-present in spring and summer – I wake to their sweet calls every morning – but they are very shy and hard to spot. The distinguishing feature is the long skinny tail that ends in a pair of club-shaped feathers twitching back and forth like a metronome as they perch on a low branch. We spotted one yesterday, just on the edge of the *quebrada*, almost invisible against the darkening backdrop of the jungle. It was the iridescent blue stripe above the eye in the midst of all that dusky verdure that gave him away.

Evelio is back, ready to garden in the diminished wind, harvesting the last of whatever is out there and thinking about planting for the coming rainy season (did we ever have a dry season?). Today, shovel and hoe mounted on his shoulder like a hobo's kit, he asked me if I would authorize Koki to use the weed-whacker in the bean field, to make easier the task of turning it all over for the next crop. Of what? I have no idea what he intends. But the fact that he worked out there for a couple of hours today, doing what, I don't know, gives me hope.

Today I swam again at the hotel pool near here. The water temperature has finally risen to a level where it's not risking cardiac arrest to dive in. I still take it easy, entering slowly. With no one there, a jungle of long-rooted plants towering above one end of the pool to break the wind, the decaying plastic lounge chairs avoiding each other on the concrete coping, and a long vista of the lake from the westernmost point of its geography, it was a moment for quiet, private wrestling with the water, the air and myself, a moment of rest and atonement for every moment that I have not consciously enjoyed of the day-so-far. In the pool I am not aware of the arthritic pain, my constant companion. And when no one else is there, it is joy.

From the kitchen window this morning I saw Evelio drag 100 feet of hose out to his garden and, against all instructions, commence to water a few small plots of sprouting greenery. I quickly dampened my irritation; as I have said, I'm desperate to keep him here growing good vegetables we can eat, and if that means watering a few carrots and beets in the dry season, I'll let it go – as long as he's not irrigating the whole field. There's also a row of radishes, four shrubby bean plants and some cilantro that has gone to flower and is, according to Evelio, attracting beneficial insects, including honeybees.

Aside from the electricity to water his plots, we have contributed the labor of Koki for two days weed-whacking the rest of the field. The grass and chopped-up weeds and bean plants will make good mulch, Evelio tells me, nurturing the soil and protecting it from evaporation. I've been trying to tell him about mulch ever since this project started, and he hasn't paid one ounce of attention, claiming the weeds grow through it anyway. So, he must have read or heard some other "expert" recently expounding on the benefits of mulch, since I know my expertise is all unavailing. He has lent me the latest almanac from the Ministry of Agriculture to read; maybe he's hoping I'll learn something. I've also suggested he water in the evening, when the soil will retain the moisture and give his plants the long cool nights to recover from their daily blast of sun. He did agree with me there.

There is a smell to the rain after a dry spell, a wet-dusty, slightly acrid smell, which I respond to with a "Thank God it's raining!" This is an atavistic response, because in no way have we suffered from the no-rain that we've been enjoying so much for the last two weeks. I had an appointment in Tilarán this afternoon, and it was close and hot in the waiting room. I said to the receptionist that it felt as if the humidity was high, as just before a big rain. She

127

nodded noncommittally. But when I came out of the doctor's office a while later, the sky had darkened, and she said to me: "It's just as if it were going to rain!" That never happens in Tilarán at the end of March.

And, sure enough, while Roger and I are both watching from our late afternoon perch on the verandah, out trots Evelio from his shed in a bright orange T-shirt, which makes him as visible as a neon sign against the blackening sky, to fertilize and water his tiny plots of carrots and beets. We watch him until the rain comes, first lightly, then in increasing strength, until finally I find myself feeling amazed (in fact, annoyed) that he is still watering out there in the middle of a substantial rainfall. He is getting soaked – but he never even looks up at the sky as the water – still being pumped expensively by our twin electric pumps – sprays vigorously out of the nozzle of the hose.

April
Crocs and Robins

Crocodiles in the lake! This morning, Tom, our friend the windsurf instructor, called early to report that Evelio had sighted a huge *cocodrilo* at the windsurf center. Roger raced off with the key to the bodega there to pull the shotgun out of its locker so as to have it handy to scare the monster off if it showed up again. Later Evelio came over to install the new ceiling fixture over the dining room table, and I got the full story.

He had taken an early morning swim, always hugging the bank because he's not sure of himself as a swimmer and he was alone. He wanted to round the point to see if the volcano was visible at dawn, but he says that some instinct made him turn back. He was showering behind his container home when he heard a noise unlike anything he had ever heard before. He grabbed a towel and walked around the corner, and, to his amazement and horror, he saw what he says was a ten-foot-long croc lazing offshore, right where he had been swimming ten minutes before. Rosa was here cleaning this morning, and the central vacuum cleaner hose was curled up on the floor. In his enthusiasm for the details, Evelio scurried to stretch out the hose to show me exactly what ten feet looks like. Then he put his hand over his heart and said gravely, "Almost a victim."

Crocodiles in the lake are nothing new. There have been plenty of sightings over the years; even I saw one, a baby, in a pet carrier in a local vet's office. It had been caught just off Equus, the barbecue joint on the lakeshore. And Koki this morning confirmed that he has seen one often, especially in the lagoon where I frequently see snowy egrets, poised soundlessly above the still green cove out of the wind. Many of our neighbors like to fish on weekends, and the quiet places close to the mouths of the many rivers are the best for fishing with a hand line from shore; such places are favored by the crocodiles. When I was working on the municipal environmental commission, I asked a colleague from the Ministry of the Environment if there really were crocs in the lake. Without actually saying yes, he said that one of the universities was conducting a study to see whether they had always been here, or if they had been artificially introduced. Presumably, if it is found that they were artificially introduced, they can be artificially removed. He also said that local temperatures were too cool for optimal propagation. I assume that means that most of the eggs don't hatch.

That there are crocs in the lake is one of the best-kept secrets that everybody knows. When I went over to the hotel to swim this afternoon, the news about the monster Evelio saw this morning had already been broadcast on the jungle telegraph. The manager told me, "Don't tell anybody!" Sorry. We who live here apparently are in a conspiracy to keep this information from the tourists. So far, no one has suffered. Let's hope it stays that way.

Third day in April, in the middle of what feels like an oven, with a killer combination of high temperature and high humidity – classic pre-rainy season weather – and we get an evening *aguacero,* rain pounding on the roof so hard that we have to shout in order to be heard. This doesn't usually happen till mid- to late-May. It brought a welcome reduction of the temperature, however, and this morning dawned distinctly cooler and clearer.

When I got back from San José at the end of March, the robins had started up. These are the clay-colored robins that one hardly notices until mating season, when they become very vocal and their distress call, repeated ad nauseam, can be really irritating. Our first year in the house, one robin thought he was seeing a competitor in his reflection in several of the windows on the *quebrada* side. He would peck at that reflection until I was sure he would break the glass. I scanned a picture of a hawk from The Bird Book into the computer, blew it up and printed out several copies to tape to the windows to try to scare him off. Nothing doing. It finally occurred to me to twist up long strips of aluminum foil and tack them to the window frames. These blew around in the breeze and successfully kept the aggressor at bay. The next year, a pair of robins decided to set up house in the corner under the eaves of the verandah, and every time one of us or the cats sallied outside, the birds set up their interminable warning call. Rosa wanted to knock the nest off with her broom, but I couldn't let her. We simply had to suffer until the young ones fledged and all of them abandoned the nest. *Then* we knocked it down, so it wouldn't be available for the next breeding season.

Unbelievably, in a country full of avian exotica, this dull, annoying little creature – the *yigüirro* - has been named the national bird because tradition has it that its call brings on the rains. It seems that this year it's worked.

Evelio proudly announced the other day that he had rescued Minor's worms. In exchange for a constant supply of horse manure, Evelio had given our neighbor's worker some of our California red worms. Minor had expressed an interest in developing his own organic compost for his *patrona*'s spectacular orchid collection. This seemed like a fair arrangement to me – and I felt an obligation to share what had originally been given to us in the expectation that we would pass the goodwill along. I hadn't known that Minor's worms needed rescuing, but it seems he'd thrown them on the ground in disgust, and Evelio had scraped them up and brought them back over here. Puffing out his chest in a clear show of moral superiority, Evelio said, "The worms are a responsibility. You have to take care of them. They need water every day, food every day. You can't just leave them alone. Minor doesn't have what it takes."

My sister's visit was a relaxed delight. She and her husband took in a few local tourist sites, met some gringos at a windsurf center party, lounged around the verandah reading, and enjoyed a cooling swim every afternoon. Alison logged some exciting new bird species, including a fabulous sun bittern at the Viento Fresco waterfalls, and we all enjoyed long easy chats in the cool of the evening before, during and after dinner.

On their penultimate day, my sister and brother-in-law drove over to the dam at the eastern end of the lake to visit the Hanging Bridges, a forest canopy walk that they described as "magical." While they were gone, Koki came up to collect his salary and to pay his respects to them before he took off on vacation. When I told him they were leaving on Good Friday, he expressed surprise that the planes were flying. Here, even in one of the most secular societies in Latin America, the buses on Good Friday do not run. That is all he knows.

One always hopes that first-time visitors see your home and your country at its very best. Although my sister had been here with her kids fifteen years before, she had never been here with her husband, had never seen the house we built. I wanted everything to be perfect. The weather cooperated; the monkeys cooperated; the birds cooperated; there were almost daily spectacular views of the volcano; and, just as they were leaving, Koki harvested some of the little bananas we had planted down the driveway, and Alison and Dick stated flat-out that they had never eaten tastier or sweeter bananas in their lives.

For most of our lives, my only sister and I were not close. With a father who was always comparing each of us negatively to the other, how could we be friends? Even as adults, when we both lived in Philadelphia – where she had her two children, and where we frequently dined at each other's houses and always celebrated Christmas together – there was a constant tension between us, exacerbated by my former husband's excessive drinking. It took our parents' deaths – both sudden and only two years apart – to open the door to the kind of personal sharing, comparing notes, that had been impossible growing up. And we both approached this new process with open hearts. Each of us in her own way had been badly bruised; acknowledging this has allowed us to support each other as we never could have done before.

The last time I saw my mother was at my sister's urging: "She's so frail now, Sandy. I think you ought to come up." I had my reservations made within a few days, deciding to take the train from Los Angeles to Seattle, since I still wasn't all that enthusiastic about seeing my father, after his role in that ugly divorce. On the train I had a lot of time to reflect, and I tried writing a long poem about my mother. In Florida and the Bahamas, she had collected seashells, and I kept seeing a beautiful chambered nautilus, all those little chambers in which parts of my mother had been hidden away.

When I got to Seattle, Dad had already cooked up an excursion. I was to drive them over to the Olympic Peninsula, where we would do some exploring and stay a few nights in a couple of places noted for their natural beauty. Alison thought this was ambitious for Mom; she was not only frail, but suffering from chronic diarrhea, the consequence of a colon surgery, and this kept her mostly housebound. But Dad was impossible to dissuade. Indeed it was a beautiful trip: it was May and there was still snow in the mountains – something I hadn't seen in many years – and it was a stunning drive up to the heights past those noble pines, the Alpine vistas opening on all sides; and later the dark, deep smells of the rain forest – here a boreal forest but as much created by moisture as in the tropics – coldly rich with invisible life; and the craggy Pacific coast, the beach a graveyard stacked with the bones of driftwood trees. Yes, beautiful, although, because of Mom's frailty and Dad's advancing senility, it felt at times as if I were herding cats. I have a vivid memory of Mom's bright red fuzzy bedroom slippers, which she wore everywhere because her feet were so cold. And another of Dad's disappearance with the car for hours from our hotel on that wild Pacific coast in his search for a bottle of scotch. We thought we had lost him forever. There was another moment, Dad and I sitting on adjoining tree stumps looking out over the silvery, twilit Crescent Lake, when I said, "I think it's time we tried to forgive each other."

"I thought we already had," he said.

Back in Seattle, Dad treated us all to a seafood dinner at a fancy dockside restaurant. Because Alison's two kids came along, we needed two cars, and I will never forget the drive home sitting in the backseat of one, holding my mother's hand. We didn't need to speak. Perhaps we both sensed it would be the last time. Saying goodbye to her was always so damned difficult.

The cicadas are back, and loud they are. The first time I heard one shriek, years ago, right outside the kitchen door, I almost jumped out of my skin. Now I quickly grow accustomed to their dawn-to-dusk singing, the background noise of high summer. This is the time of year we have to be careful about keeping the screens closed; you don't want to find a cicada in your bedroom sounding off just as you turn off the light to go to sleep. The cats love them, and I have rescued them often, just because I can't bear to hear the crunch of their hard bodies between a cat's teeth. A cat determined to hang on to a wildly buzzing cicada is a funny sight, as it tries to pretend that nothing unusual is going on in its mouth.

In life these cicadas area beautiful, iridescent blue-green, amazing creatures to have emerged from the shiny brown casings the nymphs leave all over the trunks of the trees. Unlike similar species in the north, the sundown cicada *(cicharra)* in Costa Rica emerges every year, but some years are noisier than others. I don't know what accounts for their variety in numbers, but it may be – according to the *Natural History* – that temperature and moisture play a role in the survival rate of the nymphs underground. Local lore has it that their screams increase in intensity until they explode, leaving just their skins behind.

Evelio was right: they're chopping down the trees and scrub in the old orchard beyond our fence-line. Given the cheap nature of the repairs to our common fence, I figured the cattleman wouldn't be able to afford the cleanup; it costs money to send a couple of guys with machetes into a field as large as this. The previous owner of the farm did it too, occasionally, and we welcomed the deepening view of the lake. But this time, it means the wind will be able to rake through every part of Evelio's garden, making it even less tenable for any cash crop. Both Evelio and I observed what was happening at the same moment this morning, and he threw up his hands. "We'll just have to tack up *sarán* on the fence," I said.

He nodded, but I'll wait to buy it until I'm sure just exactly how much of his bean field he plans to use this year, now that he has access to other parts of our property. We have no idea why the cattleman would feel the need to cut back the old orchard: whatever, he probably hasn't considered that he's eliminating habitat for the deer.

The green ladybugs are about. One landed on my tights when I was doing yoga the other morning. I don't know if this is really a ladybug, but it's the same size as the little red and white bug of the north, and it seems to like crawling around on people, just as that one does. It's a brilliant, opalescent green, and I'm hoping it likes the aphids growing on the basil. I finished my yoga routine, and gently nudged it onto my finger, from where I tried to ferry it to a basil plant. Instead it turned and started travelling up my arm. It took some minutes to finally deposit it where it belonged. Why is it that some insects we kill with glee (cockroaches, mosquitoes) and others we treat so gently because they bring a smile?

I'm reminded of butterflies, of course. There was an item in yesterday's paper about the Monarchs. The ones that return to Mexico in November every year are the *great grandchildren* of the butterflies that took off for the north the March before. The locals consider them to be the souls of their departed loved ones returning in time for All Souls' Day. It's no mystery to them, but the scientists are still trying to figure this one out.

In a *cenízero* tree behind the little house, there is a yard-long, foot-wide wasps' nest hugging the trunk. It's pale gray and horizontally ribbed, obviously constructed in layers. Koki said the wasps aren't particularly aggressive, as long as you don't go banging on the tree. I can see no reason to bang on the tree, so I figure we can leave it alone. Koki says the nest is called *guitarreo*, which means strumming. Sometimes local names for things are very prosaic (*pecho amarillo,* or yellow breast, for the brilliantly plumed great kiskadee); and sometimes they're onomatopoeic (*chachalaca,* an excellent imitation of the sound of the dozens of birds by that name living in the *quebrada*). But *guitarreo* - which calls up images of a classical guitar - is pure poetry.

Evelio came by earlier than usual today to water his garden. I should now say "gardens," since he has taken over roughly an equal amount of ground out of sight on the other side of the *quebrada* in what we have up to now been calling a reforestation lot. Some of the trees we planted over there didn't take, since we had no water there, so there is still plenty of open land with only a few small seedlings in it, which Evelio can plant around.

I was surprised to learn today that Evelio has a plan to bring water to his new garden. When we bought that lot, there was an old black irrigation hose than ran through a culvert under the road where it crosses the *quebrada*. Koki tracked it to its source, which was just a rustic little catchment farther upstream. The water was definitely not potable (and we certainly didn't have a permit for it), and since my plan was to let the lot reforest naturally, I just let it go. In the huge storm that jammed up that culvert and threatened to wash out the road a couple of years ago, the hose was lost and we never replaced it. Roger told me that Evelio had asked if he would pick up a few hundred yards of hose in Tilarán to reestablish the connection and bring water to his new garden. I groaned at yet another financial investment into what seemed to be turning into Evelio's *farm*.

"What did you tell him?" I asked.

"I told him to go get it himself," he said.

I'm relieved, but now a new worry is beginning to nibble around the edges of my mind. With water over there, Evelio will be able to farm year-round. With a year-round garden in place, it's going to be harder for us to insist on planting more trees there. I remember well the day we bought that property, just lush pasture then.

I walked it with Koki, and he fell in love with it. *"Qué lindo,"* he breathed. How beautiful. He was right: it is perfect planting ground – gently sloping, protected from the wind, with good soil and water nearby. When I told him that our intention was to reforest it, he looked a little disappointed, even though he understood our desire to prevent the encroachment of developers on the *quebrada* (he doesn't consider agriculture to be development).

My idea was to plant a couple hundred seed trees in there and just let the land go. The wind would carry more seeds from the trees in the *quebrada,* and with more animal habitat, more seeds would be deposited by the animals too. I was curious to see how long it would take. Although at the time I didn't understand the process perfectly, I knew it could work because it *had* worked up at La Reserva.

But no. Koki said the seedlings would be killed by the long *estrella* grass that was already well-established there, unless he could cut the grass back. I resisted, but we had already lost some of the seedlings before he finally prevailed and I let him in there to cut. I told him to cut just the grass around the seedlings, but once when I was in San José he talked Roger into letting him mow down the whole field with the weed whacker. Mowing the field potentially eliminated a whole bunch more seedlings. I was no happier about that than I was when the two of them had plotted to level the scrub in the strip of land in front of the house that became Evelio's *first* garden. I sense an implacable cultural logic at work: as long as it's cut back and we have all this nice open space, why don't we plant some beans here? In my mind's eye, I am seeing bits of our land disappearing over time – like pieces of a jigsaw puzzle – into a huge bean field with a house in the middle of it.

There's an irony here. After my divorce, and for several years, Roger and I were very poor. When our landlady chose to raise the rent on the house near the gas station, we needed to find another place to live. One day Roger spotted a little abandoned house on what had once been a dairy farm. In the field next to it, our neighbor Gerardo (known by all as *El Feo*, The Ugly) had a sizeable chile and tomato operation going. It turned out that Gerardo had just borrowed the land without the absentee owner's permission, something he has a history of doing. It also turned out that the owner had left a power of attorney with a friend of ours on the other side of the lake. We told her about El Feo's agricultural squatting, and then asked if the house might be available for rent. She leapt into action, with the result that El Feo had to sign a contract agreeing to clean up the field after his next harvest, and the absentee owner was relieved to let us live in the house for the cost of renovating it and keeping a preventive eye on the rest of the property.

Eventually we were able to buy it, and over the years we've been here we've planted a thousand trees and raised another house. It looks very different from what it did then. Beautiful, in fact. But I worry that, if I'm not careful, it could just as quickly go back to exactly what it was.

Evelio continues to extol the virtues of a totally self-contained farm. When I asked him what was growing in what I now call Garden Number One, he mentioned a kind of bean that isn't really edible (it gets chopped up for the farm animals, of which we have none), but that is really good at fixing nitrogen in the soil. Of course, if we did have some farm animals we could feed it to them, he pointed out. Apparently, it makes pigs expel even more methane than usual, which Evelio seems to believe can be captured to cook with. And a cow would be mighty handy to provide the manure for his California red worms, so he wouldn't have to be traipsing back and forth across the road with the wheelbarrow. Not to mention (for maybe the third time) that chickens produce great organic fertilizer.

I am *never, ever* – I swear this on the ashes of my beloved mother – going to allow any pigs, cows or chickens on this property.

A Sense of History

All land has a history, and the history here goes back a long way. Satellite images have picked up old roads all over this *cantón*, long grown over, built by the indigenous peoples of pre-Columbian times. One of these roads runs along the south shore of the lake, uphill from the current road and downhill from the ridge that links Tilarán with the tiny villages of Silencio and Río Chiquito. I have ridden my mare along one stretch of this old road that runs behind San Luís and Tronadora, much washed out and crowded with second-growth forest, and it took a man on horseback with a machete to cut open a way for us to pass. Artifacts of the native people show up everywhere. When the lake is low, you can go out in a kayak or canoe and explore along the naked shoreline for pottery shards. In town, there's hardly a house that doesn't sport a *metate,* or corn-grinding stone, that turned up when the foundation was being dug. It usually has a potted plant sitting on it.

Local modern history dates from the late-nineteenth century, when there were gold mines south of here in Las Juntas and Líbano. It was rough country then, virgin forest, and the only way in was by horse or mule. The gold was shipped out in oxcarts. (More recently it was taken out in helicopters.) Gradually settlement drifted north, and people carved farms out of the ancient forests, establishing a fiercely independent, frontier lifestyle. Even in the 1930s, it could take the better part of a week to get to San José: from Tilarán on horseback (oxcart took longer) to Cañas, where you waited days for a small boat to take you down the Bebedero to the Río Tempisque and the port of Puntarenas, then by all-day train up to the Meseta Central.

The Inter-American Highway (*la Interamericana*) wasn't completed along its northern reaches until the 1960s. There was no paved road around the lake until the 80s. (It's still not finished.) I have met retired schoolteachers in Tilarán who remember four-hour treks on horseback to get to their one-room schoolhouses on the lake, sometimes in mud up to the horses' knees.

The niece of one of these teachers told me that her grandparents owned our farm in those days, and that it was a much bigger property. A lot of the farms around here were broken up when ICE acquired the land for the reservoir. Since then, the process of development has been inexorable. As long as there's someone to buy, sooner or later a farmer will face the economic conditions that force him to sell, frequently just a small piece at a time, enough to give him ready cash to get along until beef prices go up, or the weather improves enough to let him get a good crop in. There are still some fair-sized farms around the lake, but since the early 90s, development has sped up and been gringo-ized.

A few years ago a huge trailer was parked by the side of the road just uphill from Cinco Esquinas, smack in your face where the first grand view of the lake should be. It was a mobile office with the name of an international real-estate company painted in large letters on its side. This was beyond ugly, but it never opened. Instead, the worldwide recession brought local real estate sales almost to a halt. Still the trailer sat there, month after month, until finally some locals couldn't resist jacking the thing up to steal the off-side tires, leaving it listing crazily on a slender pile of cement blocks. Finally, it disappeared. How it was moved, nobody seems to know. But nobody was sorry to see it go. This little story – especially the part about getting that trailer out of there – quickly brewed up into a local legend.

We've been here long enough to see people come and go. Some can brave the remoteness, the vagaries of the climate and the strangeness of the culture, and some can't.

Some people get attached to the land, and some don't.

When I was growing up, my family never lived long enough in one place for me to become bound to the land. We lived in some beautiful and some not-so-beautiful places, both rural and suburban. From my college years until I came to Costa Rica, I moved even more frequently, living exclusively in cities. It was a little shock to realize, when we started building this house in 2004, that I've lived on Lake Arenal, and on this particular plot of ground, longer than I've lived anyplace else in my life.

You can't get attached to the earth in Philadelphia or New York. How many millions of people never do? It's this *attachment* that fires my desire to protect it – not just my attachment to this particular plot of ground, but to the whole planet. It's not such a giant leap of the imagination from the sight of a young growing forest to the image of a tiny blue speck in the vastness of the universe. So, finally, it is the sense of *place* here that has captured me and pinned me to the planet.

It is gratifying to be part of the history of the land, to be growing a farm instead of shrinking it, to be building a forest instead of cutting it down, to be adding something by our tenancy of the Earth.

May
Winds of Change

Uncontrollable palpitations drove me to a local doctor, who said I should go to San José for a cardio workup. It was easy to assume the tachycardia was just the stress of working too hard for the municipality and the several nonprofits I had been working for. I asked the cardiologist why the arrythmia, and he said I'd been born with it – just faulty wiring in the heart – and that it was showing up now because of *age*. I hate it when doctors say that. After I flunked the stress test, my family doctor slapped me in the hospital for an angiogram. All my arteries looked great, except for the six-inch blockage in my right femoral artery where they installed a long metal stent. Maneuvering that monster from my left femoral artery over to my right resulted in an aneurysm that nobody would have noticed if a small internal hematoma hadn't attached itself to my spinal column after the procedure, throwing me into excruciating pain. The emergency CAT scan revealed the aneurysm. By the time I was laid out on the operating table the next morning, the aneurysm had doubled in size. By such strange chances do our lives retreat from the edge of darkness.

(This was my first brush with death; over the next six years, I was to see its face twice more. I have observed a clear advantage in this: I no longer fear it. And it has made this "borrowed time" ever more precious.)

After I was released from the hospital (ten days of intensive care later), a hematoma the size of a grapefruit had popped up at the surgery site – in my groin. Within days, this burst and became infected, requiring daily home nursing visits. I have never felt as vulnerable – or more disgusted with my body – as this episode made me. It has helped so much to focus on things outside myself – home, the weather, the garden ... even Fortuna.

The difference is in the thunder. For months the rains come and go, the storms blow in and out, but we know that the *real* rainy season is about to happen only when we hear the tantalizing hint of distant thunder. It shocked me to hear it, on my first day out of the hospital in San José, as it always shocks – as if (and, of course, this is true) the thunder wasn't there yesterday but just sneaked up on us during a tropical night when nobody was paying attention.

As friends drove me back across the mountains from San José, the landscape had a thirsty look and the trees on the dusty hillsides stood out like exposed bones. On the western side of the Meseta Central it's always like this in early May. There everyone says the rainy season begins on May 15, and it more or less does. When we lived near Grecia in our first years here, I would watch with hungry anguish for the first rains on the far horizon. Six months without a drop of water was too much for me to take. It turns out I have a profound emotional need for green. I am happier at the lake, where it almost never turns brown.

When I get back home, though, Evelio's garden is browned out; it looks as if he hasn't even been *trying* to grow anything in it. The rest of the place still looks green, but Roger says there's been no rain "since forever," so the experience of dry is certainly relative. (It can't have been more than a month since the last rain.) Roger says that it has been "trying to rain" for a couple of weeks. This is the way we always describe the first pileups of black cumulus over the ridge to the south, the first faint tremblings of promising thunder. This *trying* to rain can go on for weeks, bringing with it mounting anxiety, a frustration that isn't relieved until that first whang-bang *aguacero* finally hits us on the head.

Although Evelio was upstairs to welcome me home, we haven't yet had a chance to talk about his farming plans. Being away for so long has me ignorant of what's been going on in my own house; I feel helpless and estranged, anxious myself for the first real rain. After this giant interruption in the daily patterns of my life, I want to get back *in the know*.

What do I notice that has changed during my life-threatening 16-day *desvío?* I am still restricted to the second floor, but I can tell you that outside the bedroom window the *guanacaste* tree is in full leaf. The female robin is still sitting her nest. She scoots off to the *uruca* branch in a hurry as I hobble over to the rail to get a little sun on my face and hands. I wait there to see how long she'll tolerate my presence before she sounds the alarm – one minute! – and then I cede to her imperative. The purple gloxinia in the ceramic pot just outside the guest room door that refused to flower while my sister was here is finally opening its velvety blooms. The basil has grown leggy; nobody has been pinching off the flowers. The black begonia has given up flowering, and there are a million tiny pink bracts drying on the deck all around it. Rosa reports that Koki has been over-watering the African violets. The bills have been piling up on my desk, and there are nine untended messages on the machine. It is good to see that I am necessary to keep things in perfect order around here.

On May 8th, it rained. The afternoons have been darkening early, and we have heard the threatening thunder, but only yesterday – just at 3:30 – could I *smell* it coming. The wall of water of an approaching *aguacero* pushes a volume of air in front of it, humidifies it, cools it, so that a few minutes before the rain is on top of you there's a cooling breeze with the smell of water on it. The anticipation is supremely pleasurable! These summer rains come noisy, fast and hard, shooting fat runnels of water almost horizontally off the tiles of the roof. Conversation stops; we simply watch in wonder at the force of it, grateful that it's finally here. I remember in the north only rarely having to pull my car to the side of the road when it rained too heavily for the windshield wipers to handle. *That's* a summertime rain in the tropics. It pounds. It beats the earth into submission. It's the most powerful thing around.

Last night it was certainly too much for ICE. One hour into the storm, as the volume of water began to lessen, the electricity went off and stayed off for an hour and a half. There are so many outages in this country that we joke: *somebody tripped over the switch; the night watchman pulled the plug and went home; the gerbils got tired.* Last night we didn't even bother to report it. We warmed up dinner on the gas stove, ate in the light of the lanterns and went early to bed.

The Big Rain ushered in four days of wet and wind, just like November, only warmer. It doesn't feel so bad to be squirreled away in my room in such weather, and I've been blessed with visitors, including Adémar, who was bragging about his organic tomatoes. I was just beginning to wonder where he was finding a market for these, when Evelio popped in to announce that he has a contract for his next cash crop – organic jalapeños. I'm thrilled! Somebody at the Ministry of Agriculture called a meeting and assembled farmers for a total of 27 acres to grow a crop for export to Mexico (jalapeños not figuring largely in the local cuisine). They'll provide the seed, establish the conditions, probably check the plots once in a while, and cart the harvested chiles off at a fixed price per pound.

I asked Evelio where he intended to plant them, and he said he'd use parts of both Garden Number One and Garden Number Two (he's not using this nomenclature yet). What has him excited is that this contract will serve as a base for the other vegetables he wants to plant. It probably won't cover any additional expenses, but it will at least assure him of some income. And he has hopes for a big organic *feria*, or open-air organic market, planned in San José for some time in August. If he can get a friend or a brother with a truck to haul him and his produce in there ... if wishes were horses. And *then* he had the temerity to say he was thinking about a brand name. Are you ready? *Finca Orgánica del Lago*. I pointed out that this means "organic farm of the lake" and that Evelio doesn't *have* a farm – it's still ours – so what did he think of *Productos Orgánicos del Lago*? He thought that was satisfactory. I will have to play around on the computer to see if I can come up with a label for him. As was so vividly brought home to me yesterday when my friend Patty gave me a skein of yarn and a crochet hook so that I could while away the hours making a little pouch for my cell phone, I don't have anything better to do.

Last night, several fireflies gleamed magically against the black glass of the bedroom window just as we turned out the lights to go to bed. To find something familiar in a foreign land, where even the landscape of the night sky is strange, is a comforting thing – especially something as common and friendly as lightning bugs, as we called them in the summers of my childhood. Here, for some reason, they are not as prolific as up north, where every nightfall they would hover thickly over the wet grass in the gloaming. There, in the dusk at nine o'clock, eyes grown night-sharp from an entire evening of play outdoors, we would swoop through the dew-damp yard with an open jar and collect them by the dozens. Dad always made sure there were holes poked in the lids of the jars so that the next morning when we woke none of the insects would have died. After marveling at them for a while, we'd release them in daylight. Why does a lightning bug provide so much wonder to a child? They still make me happy.

Evelio's got two worm farms going. I could see the second box this morning, slung under the first, from our closet window. For months, those two extra wooden boxes he'd built were stacked up behind the bodega, and it finally occurred to me that perhaps my hysterics had intimidated him when I expressed my fears of being overrun by California red worms. Maybe, even, he waited until I was in the hospital in San José to set up Worm Farm Number Two. Whatever, he's now giving tours. Our neighbor, Virginia, stopped by yesterday to see how he was growing them, and one of Evelio's brothers came over to see how much compost they were producing. There are sacks upon sacks of worm compost piled along the bodega wall, and Roger is encouraging Evelio to sell some. What's he waiting for? He hinted to me yesterday that he might sell some worms. Annoyed, I reminded him that they had been given to us in trust, so that we would pass along the bounty to others. His ideas tend to stray when I'm not here to keep him on the straight and narrow.

I showed Evelio my first attempt at a label for his organic produce this morning. Initially, he was thrilled. Then a few minutes later he came back upstairs to suggest I look for an illustration of the volcano and the lake. I cast my eyes heavenward. The second most-popular logo in touristy Costa Rica, after the toucan, is a volcano. Even the national emblem features volcanoes. I'm guessing that at least half the businesses around the lake – whether in tourism or not – use a volcano as their logo. I had found in public domain clipart a two-color, rustic drawing of an ear of corn. Its style made me think of early Mesoamerica, and it reminded me of Evelio's threshing of the beans. The clean simplicity of the drawing also said "organic" to me. Just as writers become attached to their words, graphic designers will defend their artistic choices to the death. I resisted Evelio's clichéd idea of the volcano with more strength than it merited, but I quickly came up with a solution that pleased us both: a name change to *Productos Orgánicos del Lago Arenal*. This at least says where the produce comes from, and I can keep all my pleasant associations with the ear of corn.

There was an owl butterfly on the verandah rail outside

the kitchen window this morning. It was pressed up against the inside of the glass, and it occurred to me it should be rescued, but there was nobody nearby to do it. I have always assumed this butterfly, one of the largest in the world with its five-inch wingspan, was just a moth – although a spectacular one – because of its size and the mottled black and gray coloring on the undersides of its wings. But the *Natural History*, with its unmistakable photograph, has disabused me. Each hind wing bears a distinctive black "owl's eye," which is thought to discourage predators. We see them frequently, usually flattened out on a beam of the verandah roof. Their camouflage, or mimicry, is truly striking.

It apparently struck Bootsie this morning, too, as being distinctly out of place, because she leapt up and snagged it off the rail and came trotting into the bedroom with it. By this time Roger had come upstairs and, in a lucky maneuver, managed to get the French door open just as Bootsie lost her grip on the butterfly. A few parts of the wing remained on the rug, but the "owl" had escaped.

Reading about the larval stage of the butterfly unsettled me a bit: it sounds exactly like the giant caterpillars Evelio and I found chomping on the ornamental *ficus* trees by the front door. I am ashamed to admit I may be responsible for two fewer owl butterflies in Costa Rica.

A perfect, sunny, breezy day, the lake shimmering like beaten silver. I hauled myself out to the front verandah steps and eased myself down, pulling up my pant legs and shirtsleeves to expose my hospital-bruised parts to the light. Evelio was measuring off new six-foot plots in Garden Number One, supervised by the cows on the other side of the fence. Koki was cleaning up the weeds in the shrubbery.

Cat Tricksy was rubbing insistently against my shoulder. The air smelled incredibly clean and fresh and I could feel the warmth of the decking through my toes. *All's right with my world.*

By the time I am ensconced on the bed in the morning, with my computer, books, my various eyeglasses, the newspaper and telephone, the robins have already been long at work. Daytimes, I've moved into the guest room for a change of scene and a softer mattress, so now I have a view of the verandah that includes the robins' nest up in the corner over the hammock. I can just make out a little activity above the rim of the nest in the gloom under the eaves, so the babies are big enough to be moving around up there (Koki has counted three of them). Is it both mama and papa who land on the rail with a mouthful of insect every three minutes to make sure the coast is clear before taking the final leap up to the nest? I know they're both around because yesterday afternoon I heard them both hammering out their distress call when Tricksy sidled out to the verandah. I could see the cat through the French doors. She knew the robins were hollering at her; she actually *slinked* along the deck until she was partially hidden under a table. Whether it's one robin or two, the work of feeding their nestlings is non-stop, sunup to sundown. I am grateful for the forced opportunity to watch them so tirelessly at work.

Later, my heart in my throat, I watch as the male robin repeatedly dive-bombs Tricksy out on the verandah, and the cat leaps and twists in the air to try to catch him. The bird banks just out of her reach, while his mate looks helplessly on. I doubt she'd be able to raise the brood alone.

The avocado tree is starting to let go of its fruit; I can hear it. The tree stands just behind the little house, its branches shading the tin roof. When a stony, immature avocado hits that roof, it sounds just like a gunshot, and I want to jump out of my bones. I am reminded of the apple trees in *The Wizard of Oz* vengefully hurling their fruit at Dorothy and her pals.

Evelio has the entire bean field cultivated and ready for the regular rains, so he can plant his chiles. He has it beautifully divided into 30-by-two-yard strips, all black and smooth and separated from each other by little mounds of dead grass and other vegetation, which he claims will help to prevent erosion when the heavy rains come. It's been several days' work to get all this done, but it went much faster this time since the ground had already been turned over and planted last year.

I have been unable to get any further details about the contract for the organic jalapeños. Evelio admitted to me the day after he told me about it that "most" of the farmers would be planting according to conventional methods, not organic. Then he told me it was going to be cayenne peppers instead of jalapeños. And every day that I have seen him since, I have asked about the contract and he has assured me that he was going to Tilarán to sign it that very afternoon.

I'm sorry to admit that I am beginning to doubt the existence of this contract, and I have to wonder whether it was a misunderstanding that he is embarrassed to admit to me, or if the whole thing was just pie-in-the-sky.

Meanwhile, we know he is about to plant another cash crop instead of a variety of different vegetables. And I am asking myself, just when was it that we lost any control over what's happening in either of Evelio's gardens on our land?

This morning dawned gray, both lake and clouds a dull pewter. A few rays of sunlight poked through the clouds and lit up small circles on the surface like spotlights. There was a damp chill on the breeze, as if it would rain. But there hasn't been any significant rain since that big thunder-driven *aguacero* almost two weeks ago. Evelio's still out in his field morning and evening watering the small plots where he's planted Roger's tiger melon seeds and a few other exotics found on the Internet. Evelio reported excitedly the other day that the melons were already pushing up through the soil. Where did they come from – China? Who knows if they will like our local conditions? My husband is content to experiment.

When I suggested to Roger that we might try to take back some control over what's being planted on our land, he pointed to these tiger melons as an example of just that. Ah, I thought to myself, if I just give Evelio seeds, he will feel obligated to plant them. (I've noticed that he can't *not* plant something given to him – the other day it was some skinny little sweet peppers from a neighbor in Río Piedras.) Maybe he'll even accede to my request to thin the seedlings. And if I dole out the seeds by the week, then we'll have staged plantings and fresh vegetables for more than just a few days at a time. Aha! Why didn't I think of all this earlier?

I awoke at first light to a chorus of monkeys. There must be three or four troops nearby, all of them singing lustily at five o'clock. The males have two calls, one a throaty bark that picks up tempo and pitch until it turns into a sustained, deep-chested howl. It is said these calls can be heard in dense jungle up to a mile away, so when you first hear them it's hard to know exactly where they are. Over years of living in one spot, we have a pretty good idea – and I think this morning's chorus was made up of groups on both our side and the far side of the road. I'll probably see them moving through the trees next to the house later in the day. There is no way to *sleep* through such a chorus, but I don't mind. The howlers tend to sing at first light and at dusk, the opening and close of day. I like to think of these songs as Reveille and Taps.

This morning on my turn around the verandah, I saw two of the robin chicks perched on the rim of their nest, upright as statues, waiting for the threat to pass, or perhaps meditating on the possibility of flight. Their feathers and coloration are almost perfect, although they still have that scruffed-up look, and I wonder if today is the day they're going to fly. The third chick is obviously gone (there's hardly room in the nest for two). I doubt a predator got it; more likely, it just didn't receive its share of food and so weakened to the point where the others, or its parent, pushed it out of the nest – one of the cruel sacrifices Nature makes to assure the survival of the species.

The robins have left their nest. I had been looking forward to their first flying lessons, imagining their faltering attempts to take off, perhaps hopping down to the rail with uncertain squawks before assaying the nearest tree limb. But it seems robin parents have little in the way of flying to teach their young. I checked the nest at seven this morning, and both chicks were gone; there wasn't a sign of them in the trees. The foliage is so thick now they'd be hard to spot. It seemed a little anticlimactic – after all my daily watching – for them just to take off unceremoniously like that.

But later in the day my disappointment turned to delight when Roger pointed out that there seemed to be a *lot* of robins singing around the house. Indeed, it certainly sounded like at least four. We read of a study recently showing that baby birds have to learn to sing their species' songs, and they do it by imitation, just as human babies do. It sounded like a lot of practicing going on out there this afternoon – or maybe they were just singing for sheer delight at the freedom of their first flight. I feel a little like a proud parent.

There is *one* damn *roble* blooming.

Around mid-May, we had a taste of what the disasters are going to be like this year. In a freak storm, more than 12 inches of rain poured down on the Caribbean province of Limón in the span of 80 hours, what would normally be the rainfall for the entire month. Rivers over-reached their banks and boatmen were poling down the streets of the villages in search of people to help. Once again, the government had to declare the area an emergency zone. If it's this bad this early in the rainy season, what can we expect in October?

A front-page photo of a car flooded up to its door handles caught our attention in the paper yesterday, but this flood wasn't in Limón, it was in San José, where over an inch of rain fell in just two hours. The city's drainage system is in no way prepared to deal with that volume of water all at once. Apparently, no one was hurt, but I think of the elderly waiting in line for the buses, the swollen rain gutters they have to try to cross, the helplessness they must feel when the rain comes at them that hard.

The same storm system piled into us 24 hours later. We had been watching the toucans and *oropéndolas* in the giant fig tree on the fence-line behind the house. The tree is obviously fruiting – there must have been 20 birds in there, and big birds like those take up a lot of room. Suddenly, Roger noticed Tricksy poking around in the pineapple patch. My heart shot into my mouth. We know she sneaks downstairs and past the dogs to get outside, but in the pineapple patch there is no place to run, no place to hide. There was thunder all around, and as the sky darkened, I watched anxiously to see what Tricksy would do. She wandered cautiously off in the direction of Evelio's Garden, where there are at least a few handy trees to escape into. I relaxed a bit and started to gather up the newspaper to take inside, when the first fat drops of rain splattered against the glass. Tricksy bolted across the lawn and up the steps onto the verandah. A mauling by the dogs she's willing to brave, but she won't get wet.

The storm was on top of us in seconds, the rain so thick we could barely see the trees. The sky turned a dirty yellow gray. The lightning was hurtling all around us, the thunder booming only a second later, as if we were in the middle of the percussion section during the 1812 Overture. It came with a wind, just as the San José storm had done, driving the rain horizontally under the roof of the verandah where we've installed the glass. There's a two-inch gap where the glass doesn't touch the floor, so the decking won't rot. The rain was streaming through this small opening and soaking down the entire eight feet of deck, as if from a pressure hose. The storm pounded us for an hour, and then it settled into a steady rain, enough to give the ground its first real soaking since our mini dry season. It wouldn't surprise me if we had an inch in that hour, but we have no way of measuring it here. It would certainly have brought up the lake! In the west, there was a pale mauve light in the interstices of the *guanacaste* tree, as the day shut down to the steady thrum of the rain.

The Natural History is disappointing on the subject of *abejones*. It describes several beetles, including the rhinoceros beetle, but not the one that's known as the *abejón de mayo* (May bug here, June bug up north). There are as many as seventy species of the May beetle alone in Costa Rica. At two inches long, the one we deplored in Grecia was at least twice the size of the one here around the lake, but both are equally annoying. I remember *al fresco* evening parties in Grecia where, as soon as the food was put out on the buffet, you had to dash for it, or the *abejones* would be there first, crawling around in the chile or the fruit salad to surprise the unwary. After dark, they head unerringly for the lights, buzzing like dive bombers against the screens and whacking into light bulbs with a noise like corn popping. They crunch underfoot. They're always bumping into things, as if they're flying blind, and they frequently flip over, in which position they helplessly wave their legs back and forth, unable to right themselves. They are so clumsy they're funny, and they've been a beloved part of Costa Rican *campesino* lore forever.

"How *are* they getting in through the screens?" I asked Roger last night, as he whomped another one with the magazine he was trying to read.

"They *bash* their way in," he answered. As I turned out the light, I felt one crawling on my hair. In another life I would have shrieked; now I simply pluck them off my head and flick them against the wall. In the morning there are always four or five beetle carcasses on the rug.

But the biggest problem with the May bugs is their decline in numbers. The headline *La Nación* was *Mayo dejó de ser el mes de los abejones* – May has ceased to be the month of the beetles. Three reasons are cited for this: shrinking habitat, pesticide use, and climate change. In its larval stage, the *abejón* is called the *jogoto,* a worm that feasts on roots, and farmers have been spraying for it for years. Also, while there are no official numbers on population decline, according to studies by the University of Costa Rica and INBio, climate change is interrupting the beetle's life cycle. If there are unusual early rains, followed by continued dry-season weather, the insects are cued to hatch while the ground is still too hard and dry for their eggs to survive. This has happened especially in the south, where the early, isolated rains have advanced to the point where people have been calling the *abejón* the "April bug." We had that same pattern on the lake this year – rain in early April, then nothing for a month.

An annoying, comical bug. Another future extinction. I'm sure it's a crunchy treat for any number of local birds.

June
The Garden I Dreamed of

I didn't hear or see much of anything for a week, while I took time off to feel sorry for myself. I've had to give myself the chance to get thoroughly disgusted with my body's slow recovery from surgery before I can appreciate once again the enchantments of my world – a way *out* of the body, paying attention to what's around me. My friend Judy, who saw these pages not long ago, asked me about the sense of loss I have been expressing – a nostalgia or poignancy – in my descriptions of the environment. In no way have I been exaggerating the changes; the daily news confirms that. But this poignancy, this sense of loss, I realize, is now informed by something else – a deepened sense of the limits on my own time.

Sadly, I am always reminded of that June night years ago when a friend called me – I don't remember now who – to tell me about my ex-husband's suicide, but I have to say I wasn't surprised, just horrified at the manner of it. There were witnesses from the shore: he had driven his small fishing boat out into the middle of the lake, tied the car battery that he used to power the electric motor around his neck and jumped overboard. According to those who saw him just before he took off from the ramp on the north shore, he was smashed.

The news was all over the lake within minutes. The Red Cross immediately began a search along the banks, while those with boats waited until daylight and then began to comb the small coves and river mouths in search of some sign. The boat was quickly found, but the body – headless – showed up in the reeds along the south shore days later. This was grisly enough, but a couple of weeks later I received a call from Adémar's brother asking me if there was a reward for the discovery of the missing head, because he had found it. The other horror, which I learned later from a friend who had been in touch with his family in the States, was that he had called his daughters to announce his intentions, telling them both, "They'll never find me." It was this same friend who told me that he had sold the house we had lived in, spending the proceeds lavishly on the family of his live-in maid, until he simply ran out of money. Clearly, he had planned this for some time.

Instinctively, friends gathered around us the next day to share my shock and sadness. It felt as if many hands were touching mine, many arms encircling my shoulders, as if they knew there would be some who would blame me … and there were, even though he died eight years after I left him. All I could think was: "Poor, sick man." And I was profoundly disturbed by the anger that could have driven him to make such an announcement to his own children. The memory still carries with it traces of horror. But I haven't felt guilt, only great sadness at the choices he made in his life.

It wouldn't be fair to paint him as some kind of villain. Before the booze started to destroy him, he was a bright, creative, witty, charming man. I was captivated almost from the moment he hired me (ignoring Rule Number 362: "Never marry your boss"). And we had moments of love, of connection with my family I might not otherwise have had, of adventure and travel. We shared music, books, exciting work. But he always wanted to be center stage – he desperately needed that attention – and he was manipulative, jealous, controlling, vindictive, blaming. My big mistake was falling into the Responsibility Trap – I thought love was a feeling of responsibility for the other; I didn't know enough then to realize that this is just the flipside of the alcoholic coin.

It takes a long time to write a fair obituary of a marriage. My last word on that one has to be, "No regrets." If I hadn't lived through it, I might never have achieved the clarity I have now: that the abused buys into the abuser's game ... because that's all one knows how to do. But I am profoundly sorry that the price for such insight was so high.

I lay on the sunning platform reflecting on all this under a mackerel sky this morning, sure sign of weather change. There was no wind, which made it so hot that Frieda, instead of trying to rub me to death for ten minutes, just lay alongside me with her mouth open. Together we spaced out to synchronous wave after wave of the buzzing cicadas. When the kitchen timer went off, we both jerked. Life moves on.

Now, in the still, windless nights, insomnia has company.

Wup, wup, whoo, whoooo.

An owl challenges the dark of the *quebrada* by the house. Everyone marvels at how tranquil our place is, but they're used to the noises of cities and towns. Out here the noises drop into the night silence like thunder.

It begins with the owl. I don't know what kind, because I've never seen him. But from our *quebrada* he signals to another in the *quebrada* to the east. A small echo coming back, saying what?

Crickets   playing   a   triad   offer   a   metallic

accompaniment. The cicadas who screamed at sunset have already exploded and left their empty shells in the crannies of the trees.

A distant dog barks.

Later, no matter what the moon, a pack of coyotes hurls its protest at the stars. Little Flor – separated by millennia from her sisters – still remembers to howl in tune.

In the ceiling, all night long, the bats are chirping fussily over their busy comings and goings. There is the muffled beating of wings against the small, dusty spaces.

A gecko rustles across the skylight, and later I hear the flat-footed thump of the cat's paws on the kitchen counter, a better vantage point for contemplating the gecko's tempting silhouette in the moonlight.

Even later, a small but insistent mew from the cat: she's inside and wants out. When she's outside and wants in, she sits on the back of the chair outside the bedroom window and yowls like a banshee.

The pump decides to gurgle, even though no one is drawing any water.

The wind, blowing from the volcano, sighs back and forth like the ocean, and the crossed limbs of the *guanacaste* tree groan against each other like two unhappy lovers in their sleep.

In the wee hours, a far-off rooster crows.

At five – as if he were wearing a watch – the leader of the howler monkeys roars in the dawn. He's smarter. He knows when the sun is about to rise. The rooster hasn't figured it out.

A lamp is on in my small room as my pen scratches across the page. It attracts an *abejón* that buzzes his frustration against the screen. There's a hole in the screen, but he hasn't found it yet.

Night sounds in the *campo*. I never feel alone. As I look out the window above my bed, lights out at last, I see the pale moon and constellations swinging through the bowl of blue and, distantly, ever so faintly, I can hear – beyond all the chirping and chatter of nearby things – the music of the planet tilting toward the sun.

By the time I was well into my study of piano, music was already becoming very important to me. Although as a small child I had wanted to play the piano "like Mommy," the real musical influence was my father, who had led his own band on the drums when he was in college. He had an amazing collection of 78s from the swing era, loved jazz, inherited an appreciation for classical music and opera from his mother – who both sang professionally and taught voice – and he spent a lifetime searching for the perfect audio system. He encouraged me with the piano and, when I got good enough, he would make a quiet audience of one when I played in the darkened living room. He introduced me to Brahms, Mahler, Prokofiev, Puccini, and he hooked up my first real hi-fi system (tubes!), passing along his old LPs.

Music was one of the only ways I could please him, and he loved sharing it with the one person in his life, aside from his mother, whose appreciation ran as deep as his. Once, after he installed a quadraphonic sound system, he sat me down in a straight chair in the exact middle of the living room and played the finale of Wagner's "The Twilight of the Gods" at full volume. I was appropriately flabbergasted.

I've always suspected that music is in the genes – Nature. Dad provided the Nurture, and I will always be grateful. But love can take so many forms; I have had to learn to live with this.

This morning, it doesn't look as if the depredations to Evelio's garden are too severe, but we won't know until Himself shows up and counts his carrot tops. Late yesterday afternoon, a calf sneaked under the barbed wire, right at the corner where the ground drops off, and the next thing I knew a yearling Holstein was browsing relentlessly along the neatly planted rows, head down, chewing where she willed.

This was a disaster. I called Evelio's cell phone. No answer. I tried it again, thinking maybe he was showering or putting windsurf gear away in the bodega. And again. Roger thought he might be in Tilarán, which meant no hope of his immediate arrival to solve the problem. Then, in my growing hysteria, I called Koki. The light was failing. The calf was wandering. Even if Koki could come, would he ever find it?

Koki has a new (used) red motorcycle. He got this because his left knee is shot, and the 40-minute bicycle trip from his house to ours was beyond painful. The doctor said at his last appointment that there's *no remedio* – no cure, except possibly a knee replacement, but it seems the national health system is not quick to offer these surgeries to *campesinos* yet. So Koki saved his money, and we advanced him the rest to buy a shiny red *moto* that gets him to work far more comfortably and is the envy of all his neighbors.

Thus, I didn't feel guilty calling Koki at suppertime to beg him to come over and get the calf out of Evelio's garden. He was a prince. But by the time he got here, it was full dark, and the calf had wandered off into the scrub, and it took him – with flashlight and herd-dogs Fortuna and Flor – a half-hour to get her out of there.

This morning, thanking him profusely again, I told him that Evelio owed him a debt of gratitude and that *he* should be the one to add an extra wire to the fence. "I don't want to be having a heart attack every time a cow gets into

Evelio's garden," I said. He laughed and went to find the barbed wire and staples.

Over our own supper last night, Roger told me that *El Feo* had already offered Koki three cows in exchange for his new motorcycle, that Koki had refused and that the offer was raised to four, but Koki's still too much in love with his new *moto* to think of parting with it.

Hush! The robin is sitting her nest. My eyes automatically flick up to the left when I'm rounding that corner of the verandah watering the potted plants, and three days ago I saw her sitting patiently, still as death, on her new clutch of eggs. What surprised me was that she didn't flutter off into the trees as I approached – in the past she's always flown away to a nearby branch and sounded the alarm. When this time she didn't move – not a muscle – I crept more slowly and quietly about my chores so as not to disturb her. On a near *uruca* branch, her mate clucked softly. He wasn't acting alarmed either.

The next day I saw the female again, in almost exactly the same position, and again she didn't move at my approach. I snatched the binoculars from the shelf just inside my office door and focused in tightly enough to be able to spot any movement, but there wasn't even the flicker of an eye. Our houseguests, Germán and Lucía, were having a late lunch at the table near the corner, and I asked them not to make any sudden moves. As I looked on through the binoculars, I expressed to them the fear that maybe she had died – maybe there is some new avian flu that hasn't been heard from yet – it was so unusual for the birds not to be shrieking with all this activity on the verandah. Lucía suggested that maybe, after successfully raising a brood in the same nest, the birds no longer see us as a threat. I thought this unlikely, but when, even on the following day, the female – who had obviously changed positions – still didn't take alarm when I came near, I wondered if perhaps Lucía was right. What a lovely idea!

I hope the nest holds up. There were no visible home improvements in between broods, and it's looking pretty shabby.

We had a rare sighting of a group of five or six *chachalacas* in the *lengua de vaca* trees just at the edge of the garden. Since these are *quebrada* birds – they like stream beds and dark, low forest cover – I was surprised to see them out in the open like this … until one dropped heavily down from a branch and started to peck at the soil where Evelio has just planted his rice. Oops.

I love the *lengua de vaca* trees. I first noticed them along the side of the road in Sabalito when I was riding up to the wind plant every day to give English lessons. The driver told me their name (cow's tongue!) and that they made a good windbreak. Sabalito is on a windy slope (we call it Hurricane Heights) leading up to the Divide, where two of the biggest wind farms are, and many residents have planted *lenguas de vaca* along their fence-lines to protect their gardens. The lichened trunks are wind-twisted, the narrow, pointed leaves a sage green on top and a pale gray underneath, so that when the wind tosses the foliage, the trees change color. In spring, they abound with tiny white flowers. I tried without luck to start a cutting for bonsai, but now I just enjoy their graceful "bonsai" shapes in the wild.

Somebody's been eating swallows. I haven't caught her at it yet, but three times now she has left feathers under the dining room table. I can't believe anybody is snatching these birds out of the air – I have watched them try and the swallows are much too speedy. Besides, Frieda's too fat, both she and Tricksy are getting on in years, and Bootsie never catches anything but a stationary cicada, moth, or butterfly. It must be that the birds are swooping under the verandah roof and, unable to see the glass on the north side, stunning themselves against it and falling to the deck, where one of the cats retrieves them for lunch.

The expanse of glass is huge, a total of ten large sliding windows set between the posts that support the verandah roof. Rosa keeps them clean to the point of invisibility, even to me (I have banged against them more than once). From the outside on a sunny day, they reflect the surrounding countryside: trees, clouds, lake. From the inside, they look just like outside. Apart from protecting that corner of the house from the weather, we wanted to retain the spectacular view. I have seen big windows like these at tourist lodges, where they paste or paint a large black raptor shape on the glass to scare away the birds. I'm going to have to come up with something.

I know people who won't keep cats because they kill birds. In the long view, cats and birds are both part of the same food chain that we are. We eat chickens. In another life I also ate pheasant, quail, dove, capon, duck, goose, turkey, and Cornish hen, some of these killed in the wild. But we also enjoy the company of cats. What to do? We have created, and are still creating, more avian habitat, which results in more birds. As far as I know we haven't attracted any wild cats, but as the habitat grows, this could happen too. So, for now, "more birds" means more accidental food for at least one domestic cat. Sometimes, it's hard to be comfortable with the long view.

The day before she left, our guest Lucía did some laundry and hung it out on the clothesline to dry. We were chatting in the living room when Koki came upstairs to the front door to ask if he could leave an hour early. I said yes, and then Lucía asked him if it was going to rain. He said he was sure it was.

"When?" she asked.

He looked sagely up at the sky and said, "In an hour and a half."

I turned back to the living room as he clomped down the wooden steps, and it wasn't a minute later that he hollered, *"¡Ropa!"* – clothes – and we heard the first fat raindrops pelting the roof. Lucía dashed downstairs, and Koki helped her to bring them in, while I laughed to myself about the value of trusting weather forecasting to *campesino* wisdom.

Meanwhile, the professional prognosticators are telling us it's an El Niño year, which means less rain on the Pacific slope and more rain on the Caribbean. Being just over the Continental Divide on the Caribbean side, we'll see more rain. But there's an interesting twist to the forecast this year: more intense storms with heavier rainfall, but less rain overall and longer dry spells between storms. It certainly seems to be holding so far. We go for days without rain and then have two or three days of sodbusters. Now we're coming up on the Little Summer of Saint John *(el veranillo de San Juan),* which usually means up to two weeks of sunny weather with no rain at all, and Evelio has two-thirds of his field planted. I'm curious to see how he plans to water all this.

When we lived near Grecia, you could set your watch by the daily rains, consistently right after lunch. This is one of the reasons country people have always come to work at six in the morning – they're assured of getting most of a day's work in before the pounding rains begin. It took an adjustment of our biological clocks to accommodate to this practice, but we soon learned to get up with the sun and do all our important outdoor chores – including going to town for errands – before noon. Even though the weather around Lake Arenal is less predictable, these *campesino* habits have stuck, and I find I prefer the quiet afternoons for writing, reading, tending the plants on the verandah and preparing our supper. And, of course, when you get up with the sun, you're ready for bed by eight or nine at night. This is not a country for night owls.

Over 20 years ago, we regularly read the weekly English-language *Tico Times*, since our Spanish wasn't up to reading a local-language newspaper, so I can't say if the weather "forecasts" in *La Nación* were any better, but in those days in the "*TT*," as everyone called it, the weather column only offered a summary of *last week's* weather.

After a dull morning, the sun came gloriously out, and I was lured outdoors and up the little stone "path to nowhere" through the rock garden to sit once again under the *jocote* tree. At midday, the dappled sunlight felt warm on my skin, and I had to lift my arm to shade my eyes as I looked up into the lacy foliage. Amazing, I thought, it's already fruiting, and I had a sudden sense of a huge chunk of time passed (and lost) since I'd seen this tree in fruit so many months ago. They're not ripe yet, just inch-long, pear-shaped, bright green nuggets waiting a few more weeks for the Red-lored Parrots to discover them. They have an apple-like crunch and musty sweetness that our previous dogs loved. I wonder if Fortuna and Flor will like them as much? On the same broad branch of the *jocote*, the same drunken bromeliad has all but fallen over, now all dried and browned, its pods blown out, seeds long ago released to the wind. Considering the amount of wind it has survived since I first saw it bloom, I'd have to say a bromeliad is a sturdy plant indeed. I, too, have survived a big wind in my life – only one of many, to be sure – but it would be nice to think I have learned some lessons about facing such winds with more grace and equanimity than I have demonstrated so far.

Tricksy is having a really good time terrorizing the robins. No matter where I am in the house, I know when she is out on the verandah near the nest because the male kicks up such a noisy fuss. The other day, I was doing yoga on the opposite side of the house, and Tricksy came dashing around the corner with the male in hot pursuit, flying under the roof and swooping out over the rail, almost skimming the cat's back. To her it's a game – with a potential tasty treat at the end. Her mere presence entices the male to action, and then she gets to run and then leap to try to catch him in the middle of a dive. She knows I don't like this bird-torturing side of her character. Yesterday I was reading in my office chair, from which I have a view through the French doors onto the verandah, with the *corteza amarillo* beyond. I was amazed when, for the first time ever, that robin landed on the verandah rail right outside my office and started hollering at *me*. I knew Tricksy had to be out there, so I called her name in that low, threatening voice I use when I'm trying to convey that her behavior doesn't please me. Seconds later, she appeared at the French doors from the direction of the nesting corner, wearing her "Who, me?" look.

It's pretty hard for me to accept that this pair of robins

recognizes me, but what other conclusion can I draw? The female regularly lets me water the plants near her nest with barely a flutter. I do it slowly and quietly so as to disturb her less, but she knows I am there – just as her mate knows, because I hear him clucking in a tree nearby. Even when the cats are with me when I'm watering now, nobody sets off any alarms. Could they possibly feel my good intentions toward them? At some very profound level, all life is connected.

Years ago, I had an extraordinary experience with three young sea lions in the Galápagos. I was snorkeling and had paddled away from the group and the tour guide. Suddenly, the large, dark eyes of a sea lion appeared on the other side of my snorkel mask. We both hung there, suspended in the water for what seemed like forever, looking into each other's eyes. The words I WISH YOU NO HARM boomed in my head, so loudly that I really, at that moment, didn't know if I heard them out loud or just thought them. But a moment later, the sea lion swooped under me and within seconds two others had joined us, and I found myself in the middle of a sea lion game. They were swirling up, down and all around me, brushing against me, blowing bubbles in my face. I tried to maneuver myself in the water to keep my eyes on them, but they were too fast. It was delightful. I laughed out loud in my snorkel tube and accidentally sucked in a mouthful of seawater. When I surfaced and pulled off my gear, I was filled with the purest joy I had ever felt in my life.

This experience is not unique to me. I have since read accounts of other people interacting with porpoises and whales and having similar feelings of *oneness*. But these only serve to prove to me that what I experienced was real, that I indeed stepped over the edge of wildness and touched – for a fleeting, precious moment – another. It was magical, and it has shaped all my encounters with the natural world ever since.

It was not long after that experience of another world

that I chose to completely uproot and physically move to Costa Rica – another language, another culture, another country. Even if subconsciously at the time, I wanted to open my life up to more experiences of the *other*. Innately I knew that there was a lot more to be lived out there in the world than I had been allowing myself so far. And I have become convinced that it's only when we open up completely to the *other* that we become most truly ourselves.

On the longest day of the year, there were two deer at that magical moment of dusk, moving timidly through the tall grass and seedlings between the *quebrada* and the fenceline, a female and her yearling fawn. We watched breathlessly as they melted through the fence and on down the hill toward the lake. The trees we've planted in that field are giving the deer more cover. Maybe now we'll see more of them.

It is wonderful how, seemingly overnight, a brown field greens. It looked from the kitchen window as if Evelio had a lot of different things coming up in Garden Number One. I asked him for a tour and, boy, am I impressed! Somehow he has been persuaded to abandon the idea of a cash crop. Somewhere the contract to grow hot chiles for export has disappeared. He indeed has planted rice, the seed acquired from Rosa's father. Then there are red beans, pinto beans (seeds from his father), black beans, Roger's melons and an imported corn called "honey sweet." He has cucumbers coming, mustard greens, and fat red radishes, of which he pulled six for me to take to the kitchen. There are sweet red and green chiles, two kinds of lettuce, cabbage, two patches of green beans planted two weeks apart, zucchinis, red onions, *ayotes* and another kind of pumpkin. There's a whole row of *yuca* plants (the tuber, not the one that looks like a century plant, which is spelled with two *c*'s) from plants he found in an old abandoned plantation in the forest, now much overgrown but full of seeds ("*Really* organic," Evelio said), and these bushy plants are serving as a windbreak for the corn. There are the inevitable plots of cilantro, two different kinds. In addition, he has planted several what he calls *plantas de olor,* smelly plants that repel insects – rosemary and something called *ruda* that I don't recognize. Many of these types of plants have medicinal uses, he pointed out, and he wants to find and plant more. Squirreled away in shady corners are nursery bags with other unnamed sproutings, and there are still sections of the field left for future plantings.

I am truly amazed at him. From a man driven by dollar signs in his eyes, he has become the archetypal organic gardener: open to experimentation; accepting that there will be the inevitable losses to birds, weather, and insects; trying things he's never planted before (like the strange bush that produces an oily seed that is used to make biofuel); planting a large variety to encourage a broad genetic mix; using smaller plots to minimize his risks. This morning he called it *agricultura artisanal,* artisan farming. This new term seems to lend what he's doing more cachet. He seems less anxious, too. I think he's having more fun.

And he's thinning the radishes.

This is the garden I dreamed of.

He would have kept me walking up and down his rows all morning, but after half an hour the sun drove me indoors. I will put a radish and a tiny red chile (he insists they're sweet) in my salad for lunch. Only one anxious note: the leaf-cutter ants have taken over an unplanted area of the garden in the shade of a tree whose leaves they are systematically decimating. They're just starting, but there are already five or six holes leading to their nest, and I reminded Evelio that if he dumps Malathion into them, this part of his garden will never be organic. He was conscious of this and said he didn't mind poisoning their holes on the neighbor's property, but he was loath to do it here. I suggested he call Ed Bernhardt, the organic gardening maven down south, to find out what he uses.

Evelio asked me yesterday if I would "let all the gringos know" that we have organic radishes for sale. As it happens, I have a mailing list of about fifty names, members of the Ladies of the Lake, a luncheon club that takes on projects for the community good. But before using it, first I felt it necessary to establish that I personally would not be selling his vegetables; second, that he needed to pick a couple of days – Tuesdays and Fridays, say – when he was sure to be here between such-and-such hours in order to receive clients and when I would leave the gate open; and third, what was the cost of the radishes?

All that fixed, I sent out an email to everybody with the bold red headline: *Organic Radishes, 10 for ¢500.* Only one response so far, from someone who wanted to change her email address.

Later in the day, I thought I'd better go out to the garden to collect a few radishes for myself, before any possible *rush* on radishes. There weren't three dozen of the things in the ground. How did he expect to sell to so many people? Once again, Evelio's pie-in-the-sky dreaming has prevailed over all reason. Next time he asks me to promote something, I'll go outside and check on available quantities before I do.

But he did have his first client today, Barbara, the artist

from across the road. I saw him giving her the tour, so no doubt she'll be back as more and more vegetables ripen, and she'll become a regular.

When the first red-lored parrots fly over in twos and threes, always easterly, my ears still remember the calls of the Canada geese on their southward run in the autumns of the north. Philadelphia is on the Great Eastern Flyway and, even in the center of the city, the call of the geese overhead reminded us of the wild places and cold sunsets on Chesapeake Bay. It was a haunting, hollow sound, a sound of echoes and lost places. My brain is still hard-wired to recognize those sounds and memories, even after so many years in a tropical country, far from the wintering grounds of the geese. And it takes me a day or two to realize that what I'm hearing is a bird the color of new leaves with a blunt head and a red patch above its beak that loves to gather by the hundreds in the trees and shake them to death while noisily deliberating what to do next. A large flock of parrots cased the *jocote* today and determined, after a few raucous minutes, that the fruit wasn't ready yet, and so they peeled off, some landing in the tops of the three eucalyptus trees next to the house, bending the slender topmost branches like a big wind, until they continued on their way.

In the North, the flights of the geese always pulled at me in a particular way, made me ache for other destinations, a less complicated life. They called to me of a simpler, richer time, a freedom and a dignity that our modern lives had lost.

The parrots harken to the same impulse in me, except that now I smile at the birds, at their noisy antics, and at my old associations, and I am reminded that what I have chosen for myself is a life infinitely richer than what I had before.

July
Evelio vs. Nature, Round Three

During my teens and twenties, my mother was so withdrawn most of the time that she seemed to exist only in the margins of my life. Except for some noisy fights, we had few interactions. When she co-chaperoned my student group in Europe after my high school graduation, however, we declared a truce, and I discovered what a great traveler my mother was. She was intellectually curious, spent hours listening to language LPs, mapped out walking tours of the major cities. I quickly learned that if I wanted to see Europe I should stick with Mom. It was an all-too-brief respite.

There was one other way, though, aside from travel, in which my mother and I always could relate to each other, and that was the written word. I remember her painstakingly teaching me my letters before I was five. She knew her father adored his first grandchild, just as she had adored him. She would write letters to him for me to copy over in my small, uncertain hand. Some of these still exist, as well as a few of his to me, always illustrated with tiny drawings among the words.

She read aloud to us almost from birth and created in both my sister and me the lifelong habit of reading. Before I could read myself, I would sit huddled up against my mother on the sofa as she read me all the children's classics. At three, I could recite the whole of *Cinderella* in the bathtub. My mother was a dreamer.

By the time I was in my teens, she had me reading Jane Austen and was taking an active interest in all my school papers – including helping me to improve them. Sentence structure and paragraph, essay form, logic: She was my first English teacher, and she *knew* I would someday be a writer.

My sister and I still mourn the fact that the booze got in the way of any greater intimacy with Mom. Of course, there are always many versions of history, and with each death a version is lost. Our mother's version – at least as far as her daughters know – died with her.

For years, my feelings about my mother were mostly focused on my desire not to be like her. My father reinforced this, of course, in his effort to pull me closer to him. He wanted me on his side, and that's where I stayed, for too long. I was living in New York City when the women's movement was reaching fever pitch and nobody wanted to be like their housewife mothers. Alone and discovering the special cachet of living in Manhattan, I decided my life would be about career instead of marriage and raising a family.

I didn't really start to see Mom until she almost died of a perforated ulcer just after my ex-husband and I had moved to Costa Rica. I flew up to Florida, ostensibly to help Dad, and stayed for the full month that my mother was in the hospital. She looked so frail and white, her skin stretched tightly over her bones. I visited her every day, and one day she took my hand and said, "I've decided that I want to live." That's when my heart opened up.

Her hospital stay coincided with her 70th birthday, and my husband suggested that, for a birthday present, he and Dad should collaborate to send us wherever Mom wanted to travel. This was like the tap of the wand of the fairy godmother, and every day on the way to the hospital I would stop at a travel agent and pick up brochures from all over the planet. Mom and I pored over these and had long excited conversations about the possibilities, but eventually she settled on a small converted rectory in the tiny French town of Crillon le Brave, where we would stay the entire three weeks, making day trips around Provence in a rental car. Again, she researched every place we visited, including the restaurants, meticulously, and, great traveler that she was, she even packed a small collapsible cooler, corkscrew, and a sharp knife for cutting bread or cheese. Many days, we simply picnicked by the side of the road – once even in an ancient cemetery.

I had hoped that the trip would allow us finally to talk openly about our family and all its dysfunctions, but the only thing she admitted to me was that, after her mastectomy, Dad had told her he no longer found her attractive. What I finally realized was that Mom had buried so much so deeply for so long that she had no access to her real feelings. I knew she'd been abused as a child by her mother, and it began to seem to me that in my father she had chosen the only thing she knew. And she had quietly, very systematically, and self-destructively rebelled.

I think of my mother often. Every time I put on her red knit shawl. Every time I sauté mushrooms. Whenever I look around this beautiful house and wish she could have seen it. She loved designing houses, spent untold hours bent over graph paper laying out the "perfect house." (I learned a lot about house-planning from her.) I know she would have loved this one, so I feel her presence in it in some way, and this helps to fill my house with love.

I took my first walk down to the gate in over two months today, just as the sky was darkening and thunder was threatening over the ridge. I saw a line of leaf-cutter ants crossing the driveway, so when I got back to the house I sought out Koki, who was weeding the shrubbery, and I asked him to get after them. "We're out of Malathion," he said, meaning that tomorrow I must go into town for more.

Of course, I was in town this morning and could have picked it up then, thus saving a special trip and the gasoline to get there, but no. No one wants to admit we need anything, because they know we'll get upset. Of course we get upset! The only one who has the courage to anticipate such needs is Rosa, who can't wash windows if there's nothing to wash them with. Koki and Evelio haven't discovered this essential logic yet.

This time, before I could even change my facial expression to one of annoyance, Koki went on to shift the blame and told me Evelio had just used up the last of the Malathion on the new leaf-cutter nest *in the organic vegetable garden.* I sank down on the nearby concrete bench, completely overwhelmed. Hadn't Evelio and I just *had* this conversation? Did he not understand what the agronomist at MAG had said about the international requirement of three years chemical-free before a piece of land could be certified organic? Did he think that the chemical would somehow stay *in just one little spot* and not contaminate the plants growing only two yards away? Or was he just continuing to discount everything I ever said to him?

I was mad, but I took a deep breath and tried to gather my forces. It certainly wasn't Koki's fault. He's not the one who's been studying up on the organic "artisan" farming of his forefathers. So I explained it to him: the requirements of the international organic standards board; the fact that Malathion is a lethal poison (viz. *Silent Spring*); that it would be another three years before the land around that little chemical injection could be considered organic, that it didn't matter how little they had used. And I finished up with, "And *we're* not buying chemicals for *Evelio* to use on *his* farming project." That, at least, got through to him. Money, even somebody else's, talks.

I came back into the house almost beside myself. But I know that there is no way I can yell at Evelio either. Yelling out one's frustrations is not the way of this culture. This coin has two sides. One is that you have to work patiently to reach consensus for the common good, and you have to be seen at least to make the effort. Nobody sets himself or his values above anybody else's, and anybody who loses his temper is considered to be not only "losing control," but brutish. The other is that there's a lot of passive-aggressive behavior in Costa Rica, particularly addressed at people who don't know how to hold their temper. An apocryphal moment for me was when my ex-husband shouted, "Thieves!" at the cashier's window at Customs when they tried to charge us duty for some family photos, a home video and some IRS forms my parents had sent us. The window slammed down. Period.

The art of direct confrontation has been educated away in a country that hasn't had a standing army since 1949 and, since the awarding of the Nobel Peace Prize to Oscar Arias, twice president of Costa Rica, the inculcation, even at the kindergarten level, of a culture of peace.

Fortunately for Evelio, I am armed with two things. One is an amazing YouTube video in which a group of scientists fills a leaf-cutter ants' nest with cement and then, like archeologists, painstakingly excavates around it, revealing a nest sixty feet across and six deep; the other is the gentle reminder (oh, how I have to try to be calm!) that we had agreed not to use chemicals in the garden, and that this is our property, not his.

Of course, when I had this conversation with Evelio, he threw the blame back on Koki. Then he said he would plant things only for his own consumption in that part of the garden. Finally he said that it was a new ants' nest and hadn't had the chance to extend very far, so the damage was contained. And then (to distract me?) he went on to describe conditions in the banana lands where he had worked 20 years ago. Workers would carry big sprayers on their backs and pump poisonous chemicals up into the leaves over their heads, wearing no protective clothing. For the aerial spraying, workers had to stand along the rows with uplifted colored flags to signal the pilots where to let loose their venom. Again, no protective equipment. He told me that in his father's generation, they used to rub Malathion into the children's heads to get rid of lice. He told me these things so that I understood that *he* understood that these chemicals were dangerous (maybe also to show me that he had survived all that, so how dangerous could they be?). But at no point did he acknowledge that he had broken our agreement or betrayed the organic idea.

About the scale of the ants' nest in the video he just said, "Incredible. These ants are truly man's enemy."

Together, we looked in the organic gardening book to see how Ed Bernhardt deals with them – he recommends burning them out with kerosene.

That was a white-collared manakin I saw in the "compound tree" down at the creek when I looked up from the leaf-cutter ants marching across the driveway. Bright yellow breast, velvety black cap, almost no tail, just as perky as you please. Incredibly, I'd never seen him before. What other wonders have I been missing these last few months?

Walking back up to the house with the paper, I felt a moment of despair as I plodded along between the sad rows of *robles*. Some still bear the half-eaten leaves of last year, some are totally leafless, a few sprout buds at the ends of their branches, and fewer still are fully leafed. What a disappointing avenue I've made! Why aren't they all working *together?*

I've been reading about the history of the banana lands along the Caribbean coast. I'll never forget the first time I saw them: mile upon mile of cloned banana plants, all looking exactly the same, marching in perfect rows alongside drainage ditches, with cables strung between them for shuttling the heavy fruited stems along to their collection point. All the plants had insecticide-impregnated blue plastic bags around the ripening bananas, and there were blue bags all over the ground and in the ditches. Not properly disposed of, the blue bags washed out to sea, where returning sea turtles would mistake them for jelly fish and strangle on them. In those years, we read that a group of banana workers sued a U.S. chemical company for exposure to a substance that had made them sterile.

Oh, it's a long, sad, brutal – and very political – history, the history of the banana. Because it's a single-variety monoculture, people eat the same banana all over the world. This isn't to say that there aren't different varieties – what's produced in Israel may be different from what's shipped out of Honduras, say – but only a few are suited for big agriculture and long-distance shipping, so there's a high probability that the banana you eat in Amsterdam is the same variety as the one on the supermarket shelves in New York. And it could *never, ever* be as good as the organic, unfertilized, unsprayed, unprotected, unsanitized, uncontainerized little bananas that grow on our farm.

With the rains, growth happens exponentially. At the ends of the branches of the *jocote*, clusters of new leaves reach out like bright new hands for light and air. The *itabos* are starting to bloom. A member of the yucca family, the *itabo* always pushes up its new growth from the crown in a

185

conical structure – like a snowy Christmas tree – of small white blossoms that taste like endive in a fresh salad. When the *itabos* are in, people hang them upside down on sticks and sell them at the side of the road. We have at least 50 *itabos* on the property, in all stages of growth, from extremely leggy (too dangerous to mount a ladder against the trunk to collect the flower stalk) to short, since I asked Koki last year to prune most of them to less than his own height. I wanted the flowers to be more accessible, but I also wanted the trees to grow thicker, bushier, like some ancient examples I've seen in old luxurious neighborhoods in San José.

There must be a thousand shades of green.

I am a tree growing. I am the shimmer of the lake at evening. I am a flock of parakeets squabbling overhead at daybreak. I am a blade of grass under the horse's hoof, the flash on the sunset horizon, the hills of late afternoon, the new rice of the Guanacaste Plain. I am the mountains in the morning, the deep forest, the underside of a toucan's beak, the newly sprouted beans, the Earth.

Another conversation with Evelio in which is veiled, once again, the threat that, if he can't make the garden pay, he'll abandon it. I guess he's not happy with the number of people who are showing up to buy his radishes and cilantro. I don't argue with him anymore, just listen impassively to all he has to say and then point out that there are other reasons for doing what he's doing, chiefly that he *enjoys* it, no? Oh yes, there is certainly that, the smell of the earth in his hands – a palpable pleasure – but for that, one only needs a kitchen garden, not this massive 200-by-100-foot plot, which, as varied and beautiful as it now is, will never pay him back for all he's invested. I think: *I never asked him to make his garden this big!*

Maybe all this talk is just a reprise of one of his soundtracks. As part of my campaign to convince him never to use Malathion again within the precincts of the garden, I downloaded and printed out a lengthy list of international requirements for organic farming. In handing it over to him, I pointed out that the missing pages had to do with raising stock – chickens, cattle, pigs – organically, and that I didn't figure he needed all that (I also didn't want to print 80 pages!). His response was to start talking in the "circle" again: how, if he had the money, he'd want to have some cows to produce the manure to feed the worms to produce the fertilizer to grow the corn to feed the cows, et cetera. It's as if he's on automatic. He rarely responds directly to what you say. He just picks up a cue – the word "cow," for example – and off he goes, using the same language that he's used before, as if I had lifted the phonograph needle and just dropped it at random onto a track in the middle of an LP. I am trying to learn not to be frustrated by this. It's just his way. He's too anxious ever to be happy for any extended period of time.

I almost didn't want to ask, when I saw Evelio in his bicycle tights quickly checking his garden this morning after the big wind last night, but I plucked up my courage and hailed him from the verandah. "Was there much damage?" And I was gratified to see his smile.

"No, and there won't be now that the wind is lessening," he said. "And the zucchinis are coming in!"

I begged him to cut me two, and when he delivered them upstairs, he said proudly, "First from the garden."

"A privilege," said I.

What a happy little moment! All the anxieties of the last few days wiped away in that simple gift of two fat zucchini into my hands and a happy smile on his face. Except that when I sent the notice out to the mailing list, I simply called them "fresh," not "organic," zucchini, and I didn't tell Evelio. Maybe nobody will notice the missing word.

The robins have abandoned their nest. Only three days ago I saw the female land on the verandah rail with a juicy worm in her mouth. Hatched already! I thought happily at the time. Now there's no sign of life at all. This nest has been so beautifully protected on the juncture of two beams, tucked so closely under the roof, that I couldn't imagine any predator getting to them. The space is so tiny that our usual nest-robbers – the jays or the toucans – could never have squeezed into it. One of the reasons we live on the second floor is to minimize our contact with snakes – although once an eyelash viper did make it up the stairs to curl around in the busy foliage at the base of one of the potted palms. If there are snakes wandering around in our eaves, I don't want to know about them. No, I think something happened to the female in the wild. Maybe a snake got her in one of the trees. In the last few days, there's been a male around the house singing his heart out. The nest has a dreary, depleted look.

Not long after we moved into this house, I heard a great *thump,* followed by avid dog barking. I went around to the side of the verandah where the commotion was, and I saw our old dog Mancha in a face-off with a large boa constrictor under the *guanacaste* tree. The snake had coiled itself up to look threatening, but it was hindered by a fair-sized lump of something in its throat. Mancha was keeping well out of range, in any case. I think what happened is the boa, in lunging for its prey – probably a bird or squirrel on a limb of the *guanacaste* – unbalanced and fell out of the tree. I called Roger, and he found a long pole with which he encouraged the snake to slide – too slowly for my taste – off into the *quebrada*.

Poking around under the *jocote* tree the other day – it was such a gorgeous afternoon – I found lots of partially eaten fruits on the ground, in varying shades from bright green to orange to almost red. I also spotted some - leafcutter ants, so I hailed Koki who was moving some windsurf equipment into the bodega, and I asked him to come over. While I waited, I happened to look up at a bright new flower emerging from a medium-sized bromeliad on the branch of one of the *muñeco* trees. It was unlike any I had seen before, the flattened red bracts tightly packed together like those of a heliconia, growing straight up out of the center of the plant. With the sun filtering down through the foliage, it looked like a torch. I pointed it out to Koki, along with the leaf-cutter highway at our feet.

Then I asked him who was eating the *jocotes,* squirrels or parrots? He bent down to pick one up, examined it closely and proclaimed them to be parrots. "How can you tell?" He demonstrated, holding an imaginary *jocote* up to his mouth: the parrot picks up the fruit in one foot (the birds are equipped with three claws on each foot, two forward and one rear, which works almost like an opposing thumb), lifts it to his beak and then cuts a sharp slice out of the side of the fruit before dropping it to the ground. The squirrel, on the other hand, uses both his paws to rotate the fruit while he nibbles with his sharp little teeth. You can actually see the teeth marks, and there's very little left of a *jocote* after a squirrel has been at it, whereas the parrots leave a lot behind for the dogs.

From the several examples Koki picked up from the ground, the two feeding styles were obvious. But I was sorry to find out I had been missing the parrots, who have been quieter than usual. I'll have to keep a sharper eye on that tree during the day to find out when they're feeding.

Friday morning, some heliconias appeared in the vase on the table in the downstairs entry, so I must look for them next time I go down to the gate for the paper and ask Koki to transplant more of them up closer to the house. Because of all the trees we've planted between the house and the road, the driveway is becoming a more magical place to walk. There are birds galore, including an old *oropéndola* in the compound tree that always gives me a shout as I walk by. The *oropéndolas* are something of a mystery to us, because we haven't found their nests anywhere. They usually nest in colonies in large solitary trees; building complex, elongated structures up to three feet in length well out on a branch so as to be out of harm's way. I've seen up to 15 nests in a single tree on a farm less than a mile from here, but we don't have any trees like that – all of ours are in patches of forest or along well-populated fence-lines, nothing out in the open. I wonder if they're nesting on that same farm? How far would they travel for food?

Not only are the heliconias back, there's a nesting pair of clay-colored robins that has shoved the old nest off the beam in the corner and built a new one from scratch in the same spot. Getting rid of the old one must have been quite a feat, since it was so big and seemingly so firmly anchored. Who do we have now – the same pair? The same male with a new mate? A different couple? I'll be watering the plants out there later today, so I'll give them a behavioral test: if they don't mind my presence, then I'll know who they are.

The nest in the *guitarreo* was getting so big that the wasps were stinging Koki whenever he got near them with the weed whacker. He had his neighbor over to get rid of them. I don't know what magic this fellow does to get rid of wasps and Africanized bees, or whether it's simply that he's immune to the stings. I have heard that there are bee whisperers. He is certainly fearless, and we're grateful for his services.

I know several people who have been attacked by Africanized bees. In the case of Roberta and her husband, Dan, they had been on horseback in a remote part of their farm looking for a lost calf. When they found it, they dismounted and started to tie the horses up to a tree where there was a hidden bees' nest. The bees swarmed. The horses bolted. Dan and Roberta tried to run for it and managed to get to a dirt road where, just at that moment, a pickup truck came by and took them to the clinic. A week later I ran into Roberta in the supermarket, and her face was still all red and puffy. All I could do was put my arms around her as she sobbed into my ear, "Oh, Sandy, I've never been so afraid."

Most bees in Costa Rica have been Africanized to some extent. This just means that the African bees have out-competed – and even interbred – with local popu- lations, making some of them much more defensive than they once were. Early in my life in Costa Rica, I learned from an entomologist that the bees are considered defensive, rather than aggressive, as they really don't attack unless directly threatened. I also learned that the venom of their sting isn't even particularly powerful; the "killer" effect is that a swarm of thousands of African bees will "defend" non-stop until sundown. The only thing you can do is run, preferably in a zigzag pattern, or dive into a nearby body of water. A healthy adult can outrun them.

African bees are very productive, and they thrive in warm climates, which is why Brazilian scientists imported them decades ago to see if they could improve honey output. The myth, according to my entomologist friend, is that some of the bees "escaped" into the wild. The truth is that they were given to local farmers to experiment with. No one knew at the time that they would take over existing populations. They have since been moving steadily north. Now that we are experiencing the massive bee colony collapse all over the northern hemisphere, along with higher temperatures across the southern United States, maybe these African bees will prove to have been a good idea.

Another Friday morning found our neighbor Barbara, the German artist, trudging faithfully up the driveway in her bright green rain slicker and rubber boots, with a shopping tote to carry away her vegetables. Evelio was here – as he's supposed to be every Tuesday and Friday from 7 to 9 a.m. – to help her with her harvest and take her money. After she left, he came upstairs dripping wet to tell me that, with all the rain, the vegetables are growing very fast and we have loads of lettuce, cilantro, radishes and mustard greens to sell, and where are all the gringos?

So far, Barbara remains Evelio's only regular client. Even Virginia, who lives only two minutes away, can't make it during the announced hours. I'm wondering if the fact that Barbara is *European* has anything to do with her fidelity to the idea of buying fresh vegetables after an invigorating, early-morning uphill walk? In today's email I knuckled under and announced that people could come and pick their own *by appointment.* This is my quasi-solution to the essential conflict between Evelio and me, which is, *who* is going to be here all day to attend to the buying public? He obviously can't do it. He needs to make money at the windsurf center so he can pay Koki's son Erick to be here (and it hasn't occurred to him that maybe Erick could hawk a few heads of lettuce). We're building toward another heart-to-heart talk, because so far, Evelio has done almost nothing to sell his produce. He hasn't even taken it around to the local stores or restaurants. At one point he told me he was going to borrow his brother's motorcycle and sell things door-to-door. To encourage him, I gave him a large plastic crate he could tie down to the back of the bike. But *nada.* He's got Erick working out there in the rain weeding and cultivating, but why doesn't he have him *picking?*

In his first season, Evelio had to learn the principles of sustainable farming over the cultivation of a monoculture crop. The weather was crummy, the crop failed, and, even though he had plenty of beans to eat himself, his enterprise was not a commercial success. Although I was urging him on, I was frankly surprised he came back for another go. This season he's doing almost everything right, the weather has been cooperative, he's got lots of beautiful green things growing and – the missing link – nobody's buying. This year's lesson is about follow-through.

The storm reached a punishing pitch during the night,

the wind wailing around the roof and bursts of rain lashing the walls of the house, denying sleep to everybody, including the cats and dogs. We have yet to see what damage it did in the garden. It's been nasty all morning and Evelio's only transportation at the moment is a bicycle. Roger has been urging him to get something else and we briefly thought that Koki's new *moto* would inspire enough envy to motivate Evelio to find one too, but no. He has bad car-memories.

When he was helping us build our house, he bought himself a little used truck. The operative word here is *used*. So well-used, in fact, that there was no repairing parts of it. The cab was rusted out so badly that there wasn't enough metal to sustain the little motor that runs the windshield wipers. I will never forget the doleful look on Evelio's face seen through his windshield when I passed him pulled over on the side of the road in a downpour. The truck's principal virtue was its cheap price, and thereafter he simply refused to put any more money into it. Roger couldn't get him to take an interest in maintaining or repairing it, and so it finally died next to his mother's house, where it continues to rot to this day. Evelio is a good carpenter, a careful dry-wall finisher, a meticulous maker of bookshelves and other furniture oddments, but he is no mechanic. There were many mornings during the construction when he'd show up late – his little green truck barely sputtering up the drive – and everybody on the job would gather around the open hood while Evelio stood by, arms rigid at his sides, scowling in anger and frustration.

So a vehicle is probably not a good idea. He likes to ride the bus. Riding the bus in Costa Rica is a social activity, and Evelio is never hesitant to engage complete strangers in conversation, although around here on the bus one is very likely to run into neighbors, friends and relatives. This and just the sheer *motion* make him happy. He climbed on the bus for 500 *colones* the other day just to transport 500 *colones'* worth of radishes to somebody. I promised myself that today, to try to help him through this marketing impasse of his, I would write down a number of ways that he could sell his vegetables and transporting quantities of them on the bus is at the top of the list. People do this all the time. In season the indigenous Malekus get on the bus with huge sacks of *pejibayes* that they grow on their reservation above Cabanga to sell on the sidewalk across from the Tilarán bus station. More and more small growers are using the bus to bring their produce to market now that the price of fuel has made door-to-door sales unviable. There's an open-air market in town on Saturday mornings ... Well, the possibilities are legion, whereas I had only one response to my veggie-promoting email of yesterday. The gringo market is not going to save him. And now it looks as if the worsening weather might make marketing irrelevant.

Bananas, bananas, and more bananas. We're on the third stem in a row, eating them as fast as we can, giving them away by the dozens, and I just walked down to the banana patch in a welcome break in the weather to find five more stems of fifty to seventy bananas each in various stages of ripening, not counting the ones being leisurely consumed by a Nicaraguan grackle.

Years ago, when I first lived on a farm in Costa Rica, I was under the impression that I had to use all the provender burgeoning around me – oranges, three kinds of lemons, tangerines, *guanábanas*, mangoes, bananas, and then our share of our neighbor's beans, corn or peanuts, whichever he was growing in the plot he "rented" on our land for a small percentage of the produce. But there was no way to consume it all. I ate a banana every morning on my cereal, baked banana bread several times a week for our maid's coffee breaks, sautéed up Bananas Foster whenever we had guests for dinner, considered (but wisely abandoned) making banana vinegar, and pulped and froze bananas for future use should we ever run out of bananas ... and I finally gave up. Costa Rica is a nation rich in fruits of every conceivable kind. I read in the paper the other day that there are no fewer than forty-eight varieties of fruits cultivated in this country (that's not counting what grows wild), if you include coffee, cacao, and tomatoes, and the average *tico* eats fruit less than twice a week. Incredible! They must be interviewing only the urban population; out here in the *campo* fruit is an important part of the diet. Out here it's free.

A thunderstorm woke me at dawn, and I lay in bed for a while slowly absorbing all the early-morning sounds – the last urgent calls of the nightjars, the soft cooings of the motmots, the muffled roars of a monkey far off at the end of the *quebrada* – and wondering at first if it wasn't the volcano making that booming noise. But then I sensed the lightning through my eyelids, and I heard the rain start to patter softly on the roof. Late afternoons are when we expect thunderstorms, when the heat and humidity have crested and we're grateful for the cooling release of tension that the downpour brings. But what makes a thunderstorm at dawn?

When the rain stopped, I walked down to the gate to retrieve the newspaper. All the trees were dripping into the silence, and shadowy birds fluttered up from the soaking grass as I passed by. I wanted to inhale deeply and get the city – where I've been for the last five days – out of my lungs. The air smelled heavy and musty after the rain, laden with moisture as if it were full of extra oxygen. *The power of green*, I thought. How do people live in the city without it?

While I was away, someone knocked the robins' nest down. I saw it on the ground and went downstairs to look at it. It had landed cup-side up and seemed flimsier than it had looked on the beam. It was also more beautiful, now that I could see how fragile and intricate it was, all entwined with gray-green lichens and almost iridescent green mosses. There was no sign of the eggs, and no one claims any knowledge of their loss, but Rosa said she has seen Tricksy on the upper beam, which means she's able to climb the smooth posts that support the verandah roof. I have trouble believing this, but why would any animal not just steal the eggs or nestlings, but go to the trouble of scraping that whole nest cleanly off the beam?

(A long time later, Rosa confessed that because the male robin had been attacking the window again, she and Koki had conspired to put some sticky *papel de gato* – used to catch rats or mice as tasty treats for a cat – on the verandah rail closest to the window. Their idea was that as soon as the robin got stuck and started to holler, Koki would come running up to the verandah to rescue it and carry it off to another part of the property to nest there. But, predictably, one of our cats got to that poor robin first. It was obviously Rosa who knocked the nest off the beam, but neither of them would admit to robin murder at the time.)

Koki said it wouldn't have been a successful nest anyway; it was a third try and it was "too late." If he's capable of explaining what that means, I probably wouldn't be capable of understanding it. Just trying to understand about the *guanijiquil* pods he brought me this morning was hard enough. He said he had planted these trees as seedlings from the La Reserva Forest Foundation just a few years before. Now they're covered with long light green pods, looking like deformed green beans, two of which he brought me excitedly, asking if I wanted him to harvest the rest. Who knew? I opened one of the pods and found seeds encased in what looked like white marshmallow, popped one in my mouth, crunched into something bitter, and that was when Koki told me you're not supposed to eat the seeds, just suck off the white stuff, which is like candy. It didn't strike me as all that sweet, so I'm certainly not interested in sucking on more of them, and I gave him permission to harvest as many as he wants to take home to his family. According to Rosa, the parakeets love them.

I bet this isn't one of the forty-eight fruits cultivated commercially in Costa Rica that were listed in *La Nación* the other day. How many more mystery foods are there, known only to those in the *campo?*

At sunset on the last day of the month, we saw five black vultures land one at a time in the giant fig tree on the old fenceline. It looked as if they intended to roost for the night, shifting from foot to foot, seemingly trying to get comfortable, hunching their heads into their shoulders, hopping to different branches if they got too close to each other. These vultures aren't as broad as the red-headed turkey vultures – but with five-foot wingspans they're plenty impressive up close. Fortuna always chases and barks at them when they swoop low over the yard. I can imagine the atavistic fear that such a large, dark shadow moving so rapidly along the ground must arouse. Just seeing this group in the fig tree brought all the old sinister associations with vultures to mind. It's the first time we've seen a group of them there. But just at dusk they decided as one to go roost somewhere else, and they soared off over the last silvery light of the lake, wings stationary, tilting only a little into the wind, looking more like fixed-wing aircraft than anything ominous.

August
Bare Dirt and Koki's Rocks

Down at the gate this morning, I noticed a second pure-bred Jersey cow in our neighbor's pasture across the road. Koki had told me that Minor, Renate's worker of many years, had bought the first one from a neighbor with good-quality stock. So I remarked to Koki that it seemed Minor now had a little *herd* instead of just one milking cow. He smiled and said there was a goat over there now, too, producing a quart a day for Renate's nonagenarian husband who can no longer digest cow's milk. Then Koki had to show off a little and tell me that he has a goat too, and she's producing *4* quarts a day, which impressed Renate so much that she offered him 200 dollars for her, but he's not selling. It's a good source of milk for his four kids, and he claims the benefits of goat's milk are almost medicinal. His goat is just a few days away from delivering kids, and I hate to admit that, for about a nanosecond, I had the fleeting thought that baby goats are irresistibly cute, but I just as quickly stifled the impulse. Irene once succumbed, and was later pummeled when her cute kid turned into an ornery billy-goat. Maybe I can get Koki's wife interested in making goat *cheese*?

Foul. Chill, wet, blustery. The lake is roiled with whitecaps. Rosa said this morning that it felt like Christmas, which is typically the time of year we start expecting weather like this, only nobody feels anticipatory or cheerful. Evelio has informed Roger that he is "abandoning the project" of the garden. The lettuce is bolting, the radishes are toughening, the weeds are having a field day. Erick has worked his last, which means no more gardening labor unless it's Evelio's, and he's currently busy doing some around-the-house-fix-it chores for us.

One of the things you learn living in another culture is that you are never in control of *anything*. I have a hard time believing that Evelio's passion for the land won't revive, but there's nothing I can do about it if it doesn't. He throws up his hands and blames the Internet for not selling his vegetables. The weather is too dispiriting for all of us; I don't even try to explain it to him.

The windsurf center is abandoned too, as nobody in his right mind would venture out on the lake in conditions like these.

I read that the *El Niño* phenomenon in the eastern Pacific is strengthening. This is *not* good news for a lot of people around the planet. Judy reports multiple tornadoes in suburban Maryland; my sister is wilting in 100 degree Fahrenheit temperatures near Seattle; in South Asia the monsoon is late; in China, hundreds of thousands have been displaced by massively destructive rains. Everything gets turned upside down in an *El Niño* year. It's bad enough that many thousands of people die every day of starvation in a *normal* year. During *El Niño,* the numbers grimly rise. Nature bites back. It promises to be a rough year for the chronically depressed.

While it's wet, the rainfall here hasn't been heavy, so the lake is still dropping. In a stunning display of arrogance, ICE took out a full-page ad in *La Nación* protesting the regulatory authority's proposed electric rate decrease on the grounds that, because people are conserving and not using as much electricity, the company's not making enough money. We are amazed that ICE management thinks the entire population is stupid enough to buy this logic.

I was wondering how long it would take for Evelio to sidle up to me with the news about abandoning the garden, and this morning he chose an oblique way of doing it, which was to tell me to go ahead and harvest whatever I wanted. (Of course I can, and I do!) I didn't bite, instead saying that I still had some lettuce in the fridge but maybe Koki could pull me some tomorrow, along with some radishes? And, while he was at it, maybe Koki would like to take some home to his family? Evelio nodded vigorously and added Rosa to the list of privileged people who can harvest things in the garden for free. Then I suggested that Koki harvest everything that was about to go to waste and take it up to his home village of Parcelas to sell to his neighbors. We didn't get very far with that idea, because it triggered Evelio's current complaint, which is that he doesn't have any transportation to take his produce to market. I wasn't going to bite on that one either. His very first crop of green beans he took on his *bicycle* all the way to Río Piedras and sold them like hot-cakes door to door. That was in October. What's different now? I decided not to ask.

What you resist persists. I'm curious to see, if I don't pick up my end of our tug-of-war rope, how long it'll take him to come to some different conclusions on his own. Something is better than nothing, right? But he has some level of expectation that is strangling his logic. If he can't get all the way up to that level, he feels, then it's not worth doing. Selling at any price is not going to compensate him for all he's invested, so that justifies not selling anything at all.

Minutes later, I saw him out in the garden with Barbara in her bright orange rain slicker filling up a large tote bag with greens. At least *she's* happy.

Amazing. Two days later, we see Erick working out in the garden with his hoe. It would be interesting to know just what changed Evelio's mind. Whatever it was, it suggests that all my fretting and torment over this project during the last ten months has been totally unnecessary. Which is making me feel not a little sheepish, in addition to mightily pleased, and maybe even a little vindicated. The roller coaster is still rolling.

The first time my father talked to me about sex, I was thirteen and he was driving us to yet another home (we had already lived in seven). The extent of my sexual education to that point was a paperback called *The Facts of Life and Love* that my mother had handed me the year before. "Any questions?" she had asked after I read it, but I was too embarrassed to ask any, and she didn't offer to discuss it further. I had also been doing a fair amount of necking with my boyfriend that year (he was 16 and had a car), although I really didn't understand where that sort of thing could lead. We had been allowed fifteen minutes after the movie to get a milkshake and sit in the car kissing. My father knew the exact time the feature was over.

On that moving day, my mother and sister drove in the station wagon with the two dogs, and Dad and I drove in the old Mercury with the last of our things. Dad's tone was ugly as he explained to me that boys only wanted one thing when they were dating, but that they wanted to marry virgins, and if I didn't *stay* a virgin, nobody would ever want to marry me. I would be "used goods." He said he suspected what Peter and I had been doing after the movie, and I said, "Dad, we only had fifteen minutes!"

"It can happen in less time than that," he said bitterly.

The second time my father talked to me about sex I was eighteen, and my parents had just found out that I had already lost it. My mother bemoaned that I was "lost forever" and night after night cried herself to sleep; my father spent the summer after my freshman year berating me for my loose character and calling me a slut. That was all anybody seemed to talk about that summer, and I thought I would go crazy. I came close to running away. Something in me was screaming for survival, but I knew deep down that I was bad, thoroughly bad.

The third time, Dad and I were alone on his small yacht in Biscayne Bay. I was twenty-seven and already past my first doomed marriage. We cooked dinner and had too much to drink, and then, sitting side-by-side listening to music as the boat rocked gently at anchor, he put his hand on my leg and said, "Sandy, I've always been physically attracted to you." I put down my drink, looking straight ahead of me, and stood up, the word "No" bouncing around in my skull like a terrified animal. I stumbled into the forward cabin and locked the door. The next morning, he apologized. But the damage was already done.

There had been antecedents to this that I never understood until years later. All through my teens, whenever we were alone together, he had treated me as if we were out on a date. He asked me to sit right up next to him in the car (bench seats in those days). At parties he always pulled me close when we were dancing. When I was at university, he'd come into Philadelphia and take me out for a Chinese dinner. He told me things about his marriage that a father should never share with a daughter. These confidences made me feel strange, but I was so hungry for his attention that I was helpless to define it, much less change it. And I was too ashamed to talk to Mom – if she suspected anything, she never could have defended me.

It took me a lot of time to put all this together and see that my father's refusing to take my part during that long, nasty divorce here in Costa Rica was driven by his desire to punish my mother by punishing me – a surrogate – for the ways in which she had violated their marriage. I had left my husband, *ergo,* I was bad, and my husband, just like Dad, was the injured party.

Growing up amid emotional chaos, one searches desperately for anything one can feel control over. Mom learned early to succumb ... and stay numb. But with my fierce sense of justice, I tried to fight my father's stranglehold in countless ways. In fact, I fought so hard and so relentlessly that Alison, watching her older sister beat her head against a wall, chose the path of simple avoidance and found a life as independent from our family as she could. Smart girl. In doing battle, I was the one who remained in harm's way.

"You don't *have* to forgive him," Alison insisted to me later, her right eyebrow sharply raised. "He did wrong." We were sitting across from each other over coffee long after both our parents were dead.

"Then I need to forgive myself," I said, the tears welling up as they always do.

"For *what*?" and she seemed to rise up before me like an avenging angel.

"For accepting his abuse," I said, at a loss to express the well of emptiness I felt inside, "for swallowing my chains. For not really *seeing* Mom."

She sighed. In this last, we had both been guilty, but she wisely said, "You have done nothing to forgive."

I am so grateful to have Alison in my life. And I thank God he never touched her.

It's *perico* time. Like their bigger parrot cousins, the crimson-fronted parakeets are very gregarious and they gather and chatter in the *uruca* trees by the hundreds when the berries start to ripen. On our farm, the *urucas* are ubiquitous, especially along barbed-wire fences, where birds tend to perch and poop out their seeds. The berries grow directly out of the branches, forming fat clusters that the *pericos* nibble on for a week or more, littering the ground with thousands of bits of bright red, attracting wasps and other insects. It's not just the *pericos* that like the *uruca* berries – but it's the *pericos* we notice because they're so noisy. When startled out of a tree, they zoom up and away in huge flocks at Mach speed, much better designed for soaring than the bulky, flapping parrots. Today they remind me that, in spite of the cool temperature, this is still the tropics.

Sunshine! The day started gray and chilly, just like every other day has recently, but when I got to the swimming pool at the tennis club in Tronadora, the transparent panels of the roof overhead were creaking and crackling as the sun warmed them up. It was heaven to swim in all that light. As I drove home along the south shore, the lake and sky were a shocking cobalt blue and the shadows of racing clouds were skidding across the water. I breathed in happiness! Mid-afternoon brought some light squalls, but by sundown all was clear again and we had that rare confluence of light, moisture, cloud and sunset that bathed the landscape with honey. I have never seen that color in the air anywhere else in the world.

The other day I walked around the original plot we inhabited on this property years ago. There are photos to prove that, except for the grapefruit tree directly in front of the little house and an oddly matched pair of pines, there was nothing growing here but pasture. On old plat maps at the municipality, the original dairy barn is still marked near the road, now just a disintegrating concrete floor. The great old grapefruit tree was finally killed by the leaf-cutter ants, only its broad trunk still standing to hold up one end of the clothesline. One of the pines came down in the big wind two Januarys ago.

When we moved here, it was a dreary-looking spot, a lonely little house tucked up against the mass of jungle, long-abandoned, unloved. We started planting. Friends brought by carloads of seedlings, cuttings, ginger flowers ready to put in the ground, seeds, sprouted coconuts, hibiscus branches. I planted out some of the little trees that had failed in bonsai pots. Now there are orange trees, tangerines, sweet lemons, *cedros,* teak trees, breadfruits, avocados, *cenízeros, güítites*, palms, *malinches* (both the shrub and the tree), mangoes, fence-line trees that sprouted up like magic, colorful gingers, terrestrial orchids, and flowers I don't know the names of. The lot is *teeming* with life now – birds everywhere – and to walk under the canopy here is like strolling through a tropical arboretum. What a change just a few years can make in a place where life is so insistent!

I have come to the conclusion that I am losing the battle

with Koki over bare dirt. Every new shrub or tree we plant gets a circle of earth cut around it by hand with his machete so that he doesn't accidentally strip the bark and kill it with the weed-whacker. I reprimanded him once in the early years when he mindlessly killed our only *pochote* seedling, and his excuse at the time was that he hadn't seen it. Head down, he swings back and forth with that machine like an automaton, so the bare dirt around each plant reminds him to be careful.

Bare dirt makes sense when you don't want to encourage snakes around the house – and you see a lot of it in the tropics, especially around poor dwellings where there are barefoot children in the yard. Snakes, like any wild creature, prefer some cover. At our house, Koki's solution is to cut the grass so close that it wouldn't cover anybody, which means that the weeds get an equal shot with the St. Augustine at the sunlight and are gradually taking over. *No importa*. When it's all shaved down to a quarter inch, who can tell the difference? Both weeds and grass are green.

Bare dirt means that nothing green – weeds or grass – should be allowed. So periodically Koki goes around with his wide-bladed gardening machete and cuts everything out of these rings-around-the-plants, including runners from the lawn. When you don't *pull* weeds but instead chop them out of the ground with a knife blade, two things happen: inevitably some of the roots remain, and some dirt gets chopped out too. This means that the level of the bare dirt drops after a while such that the rings hold water after a rain, which can not only drown the plant, but provide a welcome breeding ground for mosquitoes. These breeding grounds in still water are called *criaderos,* and the Ministry of Health is at great pains to get us to eliminate them in order to keep outbreaks of dengue fever to a minimum. My solution to this – given that I am totally unable to convince Koki to pull weeds – is to have him go find more black dirt to shovel into the rings-around-the-plants in order to bring the level of the dirt back up to ground-level.

But this is not all. I find that bare dirt has a way of expanding, particularly around the shrubbery. As the plants grow not only high but wide, the circle of bare dirt around them widens accordingly. In this way rings have bumped into each other and created *beds* of bare dirt. Slowly and inexorably the area of green lawn is shrinking, while the areas of bare dirt are growing, which means Koki has to spend more time weeding and filling. To get all this bare dirt out of my sight, I go out and find more plants to plant in it, but the bare dirt just keeps expanding around all these new plantings, so I may as well give up.

Perhaps it's ironic that the aesthetic of this garden has been dictated the weed whacker. When I first came to Costa Rica, grass was still cut by bent backs swinging machetes.

I got a *más o menos* – more or less – from Evelio this morning in response to my "Hi, how are you?" but I was quickly able to offer something to cheer him up. Virginia had been here yesterday to pick vegetables in the garden and, since I hadn't known what to charge her, she had left a note of her purchases in the cash tin. Evelio went off to the laundry room to do the figuring, and then Barbara showed up for her Tuesday "marketing." Evelio always likes to accompany her on her rounds through the garden, and afterwards he was much more cheerful.

I can imagine he has worries at the moment, as we're heading into the two rock-bottom-worst months of the year for tourism, September and October, when there's almost zero action at the windsurf center; he's probably wondering if his savings will hold out. I hope so, but meanwhile I have a long list of things we can pay him to do around the house and, even though he's grindingly slow at it, he's dependable. He has a tendency to wander off – to a construction show in San José, an organic farm in Bijagua – but as long as I don't let that drive me crazy, I'm grateful for his work. There was a time in my life when I lived on deadlines; here I've had to learn to let that artificial sense of urgency – and all the attendant adrenaline – go. It really does make a difference to my peace of mind.

Later in the day, he brought me two ears of the Hawaiian sweet corn, from the seeds that Roger had found on the Internet. They were just a little past the perfect time for harvest, when the kernels are round and not tightly packed into rectangles, but Evelio has never dealt with this kind of corn before and to him an *elote* is edible right up until it's dry enough to grind into flour. I will have to make him aware of this distinction, because it looks as if we are really going to have a sweet corn harvest next season. We ate these two ears last night and were ready to run right out to the garden and pick and cook the rest of them, but we managed to restrain ourselves. More important to preserve the seed for sowing later. I have visions of a roadside stand with bushel baskets overflowing with picked-that-day ears of sweet corn and a big red and white sign like the ones that lined the country roads in the New Jersey of my youth. We would cross the Delaware River from the Pennsylvania side, already salivating, and bring home enough sweet corn and tomatoes still warm from the fields to make a meal. Plenty of butter and salt and pepper, but nothing else. Evelio says that to be absolutely sure the corn will be safe from the depredations of the weather, he's going to plant it in Garden Number Two.

I still want him to plant *some* things in Garden Number One, because I enjoy wandering leisurely up and down the rows right out the back door with the sun on my back, peeking under leaves for the smallest green beans, or poking in the dirt around a dark red radish to see if it's big enough to pull out of the ground. I appreciate what Evelio means when he talks about *el olor de la tierra,* the smell of the earth, even though I can't physically do all that work. It must be a basic human instinct, since it's awakening even in me, who in all these decades has never had a vegetable garden of her own.

There was a bat in the living room fireplace last night. Frieda was stretched up against the fireplace screen sniffing at something interesting, so I went over and tilted the screen toward me a little, thinking maybe we had a bird trapped in there. Over the top sneaked a sooty foot attached to a webby wing, and I slammed the screen back in place. A bird I would have tried to rescue; a bat I will leave for Koki to handle with one of his big gloves. Bats are valuable to have around for pollination and insect control, but let's face it, they are not cute. (They can also be carriers of rabies in this country.) I am grateful the screen so perfectly fits the fireplace opening, so we could leave the bat in there overnight without worrying that he'd get loose in the house.

After Koki had safely removed him and let him go off the side of the verandah, Roger closed the fireplace damper, and we decided to have a fire in there soon just in case the bats have taken to spending their days inside the chimney cap. I learned early in my country life in Costa Rica that bats are habitual, persistent creatures and very hard to get rid of once they've established a roosting spot.

When we lived near Grecia, our neighbor Ruth had bats in her ceiling. When the previous owner of her house remodeled one section of the roof, he neglected to close up the eaves, a cost-saving measure that paid off in a two-foot accumulation of bat guano that was now sifting down through the wooden ceiling into the bedroom. This was disgusting, not to mention toxic, and Ruth had to move downstairs.

The only solution, the locals said, was to remove the corrugated tin roofing, chase them out and spread a lot of garlic around since, as everyone knows, bats don't like the smell of garlic.

Visions of Bela Lugosi came to mind. I'm not averse to natural remedies, but the variety – and often the redundancy – of these is bewildering: oregano mashed in milk for the stomach; the same concoction – as hot as you can stand it – for a cough; a certain cactus to "refresh" the digestive system; the juice of sweet lemon for conjunctivitis; eucalyptus tea for a cold; bay leaves in the kitchen cabinets to repel spiders (I tried it; it didn't work). But Ruth was inclined to put her faith in more practical measures: she got her farm manager to peel away part of the tin roof, shoo away the bats, pack the guano into sacks to fertilize the coffee on her farm, replace the roof and nail screens up under the eaves.

But the animals broke right through the screening. Apparently 150 watts burning up there night and day was no deterrent either.

One evening Ruth gave us a bat show. Promptly at six o'clock, the sun beneath the horizon but still flooding the sky with pink light, twenty-nine *murciélagos* soared out from under her roof in ones and twos, ready for their night's foraging. Every time we were over there in the evening, we would count them out loud, sounding out the syllables, as they flew out from under the eaves: "Twenty-six, twenty-seven, twenty-eight, twenty-nine!" It became one of our favorite country entertainments – better than television.

Finally, a neighbor, Ted, the retired military engineer, installed what he called "ECM" in Ruth's attic. This was a small black box that was supposed to emit a high-pitched sound inaudible to human ears but inimical to bats.

"What's ECM stand for?" we asked Ted one evening just before 1800 hours.

"Electronic countermeasures," he answered.

213

Just then the first two bats swooped out from under Ruth's roof. Over the next few minutes the rest came – all twenty-nine of them. As always, we counted them out loud. Ted stared dolefully into his beer.

These were the dark little fruit bats that are so valuable on a farm. Ruth said she was considering building a bat house to attract them.

"What does a bat house look like?" I asked her.

"Exactly like my roof," she answered.

I was away in San José only two and a half days, and when I came back Koki had weed whacked everything within shouting distance of the house – he knows how I hate the sound of that machine – working "like a mule," he said, to get it all done before I returned. Then he went around with his sprayer and killed *thirty* fire ants' nests. Everything's looking so good, and the rains have slowed so much that things aren't growing with their usual jungle vigor, and he's running out of things to do. When he hinted at the need for another project this morning, I decided to brave the problem of the bare dirt all around the shrubbery. Last evening, I caught Fortuna and Flor digging up one of these areas at the top of the rock garden, and I realized that all this bare dirt is just irresistible to dogs, who love nothing better than to make a nice, cool dirty nest in a shady spot on a hot day.

From the beginning of this conversation, I could tell Koki thought I was being silly, because he kept his head down and tried to control the little smile starting up at the corners of his mouth. I patiently explained how and why the gardens have kept expanding all these years, and what a temptation it is to the dogs, and how it just turns to mud in the rainy season and, finally, how I wanted him to plant

214

grass in all that bare dirt so I wouldn't have to look at it anymore. I even hauled him over to the top of the rock garden, and I was able to prove to him how the boundary between plants and grass has grown over the years because, buried there about eight inches from the edge of the grass, you can still see the top of the green plastic garden edging I'd asked him to place there to keep the grass *out* of the rock garden. (*That* was a wasted purchase at the nursery.) We then discussed where he would find the St. Augustine and how he would transport it all from the bank along the road on the other side of the *quebrada* where it grows naturally – by wheelbarrow, *not* by Minor's pickup truck, which we would have to pay for – and he finally looked up at me and said, "Okay! You're the boss!"

Down in the dumps again, Evelio admitted that he's not a business person. "Others have the ability to negotiate and sell," he said to me the other day. "Not me. I just love to grow things. If I had a partner ..."

But he knows a partner would eat into his slender earnings, so he just sighs and shrugs and lets it go.

I have ceased to be frustrated by this. He knows what he is, so why should I chafe at what he *isn't*? (It's taken me a long time to reach this understanding.) And just as I was beginning to fear we'd lost our organic vegetable garden forever, three new clients showed up on the same day, in addition to the faithful Barbara from across the road: Roberta, whose own organic garden has run out of lettuce and cabbage; Judy, who wandered happily up and down the rows with Evelio on tour (he even gallantly climbed a tree to pull down some guavas for her) and who has *tica* friends she's going to buy for too; and a vegan couple who eat nothing but raw organic food and who've bought property on the other side of La Reserva but haven't had a chance to plant anything on it yet. Heaven is watching out for our dear Evelio; I needn't worry about him *too* much.

It took several pickup truck loads to get rid of all the rocks in the mossy pile down by the creek and the compound tree. Before we built the house, we had to make an entrance from the road and create a drive sturdy enough to get heavy vehicles uphill to the construction site. Once this was graded, we ordered *toba,* a mixture of rock and a fine clay that, together with the rains and the pounding of those heavy trucks, would serve as a solid base for a future gravel driveway. I remember coming home the day the *toba* had been delivered. The rocks in the mixture were so big that you would have hesitated to take a car over them, and there was no *walking* the drive at all. We complained to the contractor, but it was already on the ground for a distance of 175 yards; what could we do? He didn't volunteer to shovel it up or give us our money back. So we laboriously moved the biggest of these rocks off to the side of the drive by hand – or, I should say, by strong backs, including Koki's. Many of these rocks were a challenge for a single strong *campesino* to lift, and the men had to work in pairs. It was like watching laborers on a Georgia chain gang until all those rocks were out of the way.

Once the house was built, a young man who had apprenticed to a landscape gardener in California used some of the rocks to build my pretty rock garden under the *jocote* tree, along with a couple of low walls along the sides of the driveway closest to the house. Those rocks that didn't get used in the garden or the walls Koki had to move down the hill to stack out of sight near the compound tree. Roger then thought we should have rocks in the creek to slow the force of the runoff, and thus erosion, during the heavy rains, so one season Koki and some "extras" peppered the creek bed with more of our rocks, only to find that, when the rains died down, perfect little mosquito breeding pools remained behind. We asked Koki to pull the rocks back out. Indeed, Koki has moved these rocks around so much during all these years that he probably feels a proprietary interest in them, because he asked Roger one day recently if it was okay if he sold them. Roger probably wasn't paying close attention – as frequently happens when Koki asks him something in his rapid non-consonantal Spanish, which is almost completely incomprehensible to both of us – so he said, "Sure."

Of course, Koki kept the money.

Evelio's *más o menos* responses seem to be coming with more frequency, or maybe he's just finding in me a sympathetic ear, so he feels he *can* talk about his feelings of being *desequilibrado* (out of equilibrium), which is something a *Latino* male wouldn't normally do, even with a friend. And perhaps over time I am learning to listen with a little less personal anxiety about how his negative feelings might affect the future of organic vegetables on our farm. Could I be getting used to this roller coaster ride?

So today, as a distraction, I asked him to show me how the rice grains develop. I've noticed that the rice plants seem suddenly to have doubled in height, so I was curious about when and how they would be harvested. Happily, Evelio strode into the rice patch, leading me to a plant that had already set its lovely, drooping golden grains. He invited me to lift them in my palm to feel the weight of them. This is *arroz de montaña*, forest or mountain rice, that he got from Rosa's father Pedro. Evelio has seen images of rice paddies in the Far East, with people in water up to their shins bending over to harvest the plants. He was curious about the need for water, since it's not grown that way here. He demonstrated how he will lean down and harvest the plant at ground level with a special knife he called a *cuchillo de os*. The rice will be ready for harvest in September, and I'm looking forward to seeing how it's done.

A little later, Evelio hitched a ride with me into town. He spoke more about what he was feeling about the garden, his voice steady, his hands held calmly in his lap. "For me agriculture is a very personal thing," he said. "If the plants do well, I am well. If the plants suffer, I suffer. I'm tired," he went on. "I'm going to lay off for a while. I need to recharge my batteries."

It felt like a new knowledge and acceptance of self that I was hearing, and I could only warmly agree. He's worked hard. The windy season will be upon us soon, with much heavier rains, making conditions almost impossible for him to continue. It's a good time for him to take a break. He's excited about the sweet corn, though – he pulled the ears on the last day of the month to bring inside for drying and saving the seed. I suspect when the weather eases up in February or March, he'll plant them in Garden Number Two on the other side of the *quebrada* out of the wind. "And maybe I'll plant some more beans over there," he mused. I heaved an inward sigh of relief. He won't be able to let it go forever.

That evening I sat out on the "stoop" – the topmost step of the graceful pine staircase Evelio built leading from the verandah down to the lawn. The wind at sunset was northerly; smoke and ash draped over the southern slope of the volcano like a veil. The lights of the town of New Arenal twinkled forth like distant sparks from the volcano. The lake was a solid gray mass between Evelio's garden and the far shore, the sky a pale lilac in the west. Thin tendrils of cloud snaked down through the high passes between the hills. From across the water I could hear the distant thrumming of a school band in their evening practice for Independence Day. I have been hearing these bands practice, now, for a generation – the children I first knew around here now have children of their own. In that moment, the lake felt like a very intimate place.

Interamericana Norte

The upper reaches of the Inter-American Highway are nothing more than a country back road, one lane in each direction, lined with heavy old trees and second-growth forest and offering spectacular vistas, from its pass through the mountains, of the Guanacaste Plain, the Gulf of Nicoya and the blue-gray mountains that divide the peninsula from the Pacific. For decades, the only trucking route northwest from San José to the ports of Caldera and Puntarenas or the border with Nicaragua, this pass has always been a driving nightmare. One is frequently caught in long "elephant trains" of eighteen-wheelers belching smoke and grinding their way up or down the mountain in their lowest gears. Heading north, once past the exit for Caldera, however, the road is seldom congested except for the occasional road accident or bridge washed out. I frequently marvel, as I'm taking this route, that it is the *same* route that – except for a gap between Panama and Colombia that has to be end-run by a ferry – stretches from Tierra del Fuego all the way to Alaska, in most places in far better repair than it is here in Costa Rica. Just across the border in Nicaragua, it turns into a beautiful four-lane highway, well-marked, well-maintained. The reason, I suspect, lies in the presence of a military. I am reminded that President Eisenhower prioritized the U.S. Interstate highway system for public defense after World War II. Costa Rica has no army, so it becomes a matter of reverse pride that our roads are so bad.

But back to the trees. Stretching over the roadway on the Interamericana Norte are hundreds of *guanacaste* trees, their broad branches heavy with termite nests and epiphytes which, in the hot lowlands, tend to be succulents, as opposed to the bromeliads and air plants on the trees around the lake. Many of these old trees are huge, obvious remnants of the days when this road was first carved through virgin forest in the fifties. In the indigenous language of northwestern Costa Rica, *guanacaste* means "tree of the ear," so called because of its large, flat, roundish, dark-brown seedpods. The seeds themselves, difficult to pry out of the tough white flesh inside the pods, are polished black and brown ovals, so beautiful and durable that they were once used as a means of exchange. Like others in the mimosa family, *guanacastes* are fast growers with lovely lacy foliage and wispy pink blooms, and their giant domed canopies make for welcome shade throughout northern Costa Rica, especially along the highway in what remains of the ancient dry tropical forest.

These days I go to San José mostly for medical reasons. In earlier times, it was to attend meetings of a women's writers' workshop, the members of which all became good friends. From Grecia, in those days it was only a half-hour run. From Tilarán, it turned into a four-and-a-half-hour bus or car trip – just sheer agony any way you did it. Lacking a car for the first couple of years after the separation from my husband, the bus was the only option, and I quickly learned to adapt to the discomforts and courtesies of long-distance bus travel in Costa Rica.

First was to find a seat by a window that opened. Many older Costa Ricans from the *campo* don't like air blowing on them; they think it makes them sick. So, no matter what the ambient temperature, the un-air-conditioned buses barreled down the road through the lowlands like hermetically sealed infernos. The only exception to this was when a young woman in the seat across the aisle from me threw up her breakfast just after we took off from Tilarán. I prayed she would get off in Cañas, but no, she sat there, too embarrassed to move, her morning's rice and beans in her lap all the way to San José. On that trip, the windows flew open and stayed that way.

Second, I quickly learned not to sit behind the driver on a night run. These guys are cowboys, the headlights reach only so far, there are frequently no lines painted on the road, it's dark as pitch out there and it feels as if we're flying completely blind. Not for the faint of heart.

Third, drink little and empty your bladder fully before boarding the bus. It didn't always make a rest stop. My strategy on the city run was to jump off the bus at the old Hotel Corobicí at the entrance to San José and dash for their comfortable ladies' room. One time the bus driver pulled over to the side of the road and yelled back that the gentleman who wanted to go to the bathroom could do so now, and a voice from the rear hollered, "That's all right. Never mind!" There was general laughter on board, the driver shrugged in that exaggerated Latin way and pulled back into traffic.

In daylight I would try to read, but there was constant social chatter, crying babies and mariachis playing loudly on the radio. I remember one moment, crossing that mountaintop just at sundown, the magnificent Costa Rican scenery stretching out all around me in the waning light, the mariachis singing, a general feeling of contentment and goodwill on the bus as we all swerved back and forth around the hairpin curves, being overcome by a happiness to find myself winding serenely along a Central American highway. It was a "what am I doing here?" moment, and the answer was that I was going home.

Arrival, no matter how long I've been away, is always a balm to the spirit. When I turn the corner off the Interamericana at the bullring and drive through the town of Cañas – which takes only a minute – I breathe a sigh of relief to be finally on a real back road without the pressure of international traffic. The elevation at Cañas is only 210 feet above sea-level, and you steadily rise another 1500 feet in just fourteen miles, through wide, windy vistas of pastureland and stranded, stunted trees, the rank of volcanoes Tenorio, Miravalles, and Rincón de la Vieja marching northwest off to your left. In the last few miles before Tilarán, the view closes in and you negotiate a series of hairpin curves, zip through the farming village of Los Angeles, and dip up, down and around as you skim the billowing waves of the Tilarán Mountains. On one curve stand three giant *ceiba* trees that always lift the heart. Farther on is a glimpse of Tilarán itself, off to the right, huddled on a small raft in an ocean of green. Just before the last rise, you cross a little bridge in a jungle glade that gives you one last reminder that civilization in these parts is still a relatively recent thing. Up the hill, past mechanics, corner stores, billboards, a restaurant – the clutter at the entrance to any small town – you take a sharp turn to the left, down the hill, over another bridge, then up, around and up some more till you pass the all-night gas station on the Continental Divide and finally arrive at the lake and *home*.

The first time ever I crested that last hill, the long view of the great blue bowl of the lake amid its lushly green hills took my breath away. All these many years later, it still gladdens my heart.

September
Evelio vs. Roundup, TKO

September sneaked in under a white fog, so we didn't see it until a day later, when the mist and rain cleared out, and we faced a brilliant day, the lake and sky an equal blue. We have always said that September is our favorite month here, with the greatest number of clear days and the most frequent sightings of Volcán Arenal. This is what we always tell the tourists who complain when the volcano fails to show during the fourteen hours that they're here: come back in September.

In the last couple of weeks, there has been a strangely sweet smell down near the gate, and I asked Koki to identify it for me: the flowering *güitite* trees along the road. He brought me a small branch jammed with white flowers. Individually, the flowers don't have much fragrance, but in such great numbers their fragrance is almost overwhelming. I had a gardener once who refused to cut back the branches of a fruiting *güitite* until all the bright orange berries were gone, because he knew what a great food source they were to many species of birds. *Güitites* are host to orchids, as well; the bark is deeply striated and cork-like, making perfect crannies for infinitesimally tiny wind-borne seeds. Many women I know plant *güitites* in their yards on purpose to show off their spectacular orchid collections.

The monkeys haven't been around lately. I was

reminded of this when today's five a.m. howl was louder – and closer – than usual. In dry season the howlers move along the *quebradas* more rapidly, searching out new growth on the trees, which is scarcer at that time of year. When it's raining regularly, as it has been lately, there is a surfeit of food, so they don't need to roam so fast, but have the luxury of lolling around in one spot for longer periods of time. We miss their more frequent company. When the rains come hard and cold and last for weeks, the monkeys hunker down in the nooks of the trees and simply try to keep warm. We hardly hear them at these times, and we fear for them. The cold and wet will kill the weaker ones.

Our *quebrada* is just a spur, or tributary, leading into the larger and lusher gorge that winds down to the lake. That one appears on the old topographical maps as the Quebrada Bullicioso, which means noisy, riotous, tumultuous. It pleased me when I first found that our exact spot on the map has a name: Bullicioso. I like to think of a river's roaring tumult on its way to the sea. On the eastern side of the Continental Divide, the Arenal watershed used to drain toward the Caribbean. When the dam was built, a tunnel was dug under the Divide, redirecting the flow to the Pacific. I have traced this route on maps, where it flows downhill through three hydroelectric power stations and thence into the Río Corobicí, which empties into the Río Bebedero, and from there into the grand basin of the Río Tempisque and on into the Gulf of Nicoya, one of the safe havens where Sir Francis Drake anchored during his explorations of the Western Americas.

We know that the Quebrada Bullicioso supports more than one band of howler monkeys, because we've seen two groups passing each other right near here – what a noisy operation that is! And there are white-faced monkeys, too, although they are much shyer and I've only seen them once. Years ago, our old dog Mancha was barking vigorously at something behind the little house. I went out to investigate and saw a pair of *carablancas* angrily jumping up and down on a tree limb, throwing twigs and leaves at the dog. I shushed Mancha and stayed with her there for a while until the monkeys calmed down and moved off.

Having monkeys in our backyard is especially precious when we reflect on the fact that the population of howlers in Costa Rica declined by fifty percent during one fifteen-year period. The reason is shrinking habitat and the breaking up of what habitat remains into isolated patches. Monkeys need a way to get from forest island to island for groups to interbreed. If they can't, the gene pool shrinks and they become more vulnerable to disease. The fact that our *quebrada* system supports two groups is great, and now, thanks to the efforts of La Reserva, we have a monkey bridge to take them safely across the road to the continuation of the *quebrada* on the other side, from which, along fences and tree-lines, they can get to the smaller *quebrada* to the southeast. How far they actually move is anybody's guess. This particular population hasn't been studied. Just one more reason to plant trees.

There has been some talk downstairs of the advantages of putting a horse to graze in the reforestation area – Koki's Park – between the house and the road. Koki has been told to conserve gasoline by cutting the grass in there less frequently, which makes for huge piles of mown grass that he feels he needs to rake up and dispose of. Fortunately, Evelio has a use for this grass as mulch in his garden, so Koki transports it all by wheelbarrow up the hill and to the back of the house. All of this is plenty of work, especially on a sunny day. Evelio, meanwhile, is probably looking for a nearer source of horse manure for his California worm farm. They both tried to convince me this morning that a horse in there wouldn't destroy the trees and it would eliminate the need for all this labor and the expense of the gas.

The two of them forget that for a number of years there *was* a horse in there, in fact a mare, which meant a new filly every couple of years, the need to build a shed to shelter them from the rain, the cost of feed, veterinary checks, shoeing, worming, training and keeping the fences fixed. What – do they think I've forgotten all this? Do they really think I have forgotten that a horse will destroy a good-sized pasture in just a few years because it eats the grass right down to the roots? That it will eat the leaves off of every growing thing within reach? That it will scratch its hind end on fence posts, and then wander over the sagging barbed wire out onto the road where it has to be chased and caught?

I looked at them both incredulously. Koki read my mind.

"You could rent it," he said, meaning the land.

"And who will build the fence to keep the horse from decimating the vegetable garden or chewing the shrubbery?" I asked. *De ninguna manera.* No way.

There was a time when I loved having a horse. The hills around the lake, with their rough tracks, scattered farms and deep forests, and with their stunning highland views over lake and mountains, are some of the best riding country in the world. I wouldn't trade for anything the years when I had the privilege of getting up in the cool of a morning and throwing a saddle on the back of my mare and just trotting off to nowhere. There was even a time when my mare substituted for a car and a telephone. In those days, I'd mount up on a Sunday morning and go calling on my neighbors, following a regular route and stopping to chat or have a cup of coffee. There was real joy when that first filly was born; she was the most beautiful thing I'd ever seen.

But eventually the mare went lame and, in a sense, so

did I. She was sold to Mariano, the owner of the sire that had produced the beautiful filly; the fence around the pasture disappeared; the feed shed was dismantled; we started planting trees. Every stage of life has its satisfactions.

Koki and Evelio have hatched up an amazing way to kill two birds with one stone. I confess it never would have occurred to me, so I'm doubly delighted. For years there has been a depression in the lawn between the house and the *corteza amarilla*. This was a place where some small construction leftovers had been buried (they should have been carted away to the municipal dump) and just filled in when the backhoe was here doing some final grading. Of course with every succeeding rain, the earth has worked its way around all those little pieces of steel and whatever, so over time a sink hole has grown there. I have tripped in this thing more than once, and I finally asked Koki the other day if he'd strip off the sod, fill in the hole and put the grass back on top. It didn't occur to me to ask where he was going to find the fill to do this. It's a big property; there are *acres* of dirt here to be dug up without anybody noticing.

Koki started this project yesterday, but it was only today that I noticed the big hole in Evelio's garden – right where Evelio had pumped Malathion into the ground to kill off the leaf-cutter ants. Wonderful! No more contaminated soil in the garden (and no ants either, I notice), and the new hole can serve not only as a Monument to the Malathion Mistake, it can be a repository for organic garden trash. We may need to put a little fence around it, however. It's pretty deep. I'd hate for anybody to trip and fall into it.

The reforestation project in Koki's Park is finally beginning to take off on its own, or rather, is proving that it's going to be *able* to take off on its own. Koki pointed out to me a bright, beautiful, lacy-green *guachepelín* seedling about a foot high that has popped up in a grove where the foliage is dense enough to keep the grass from growing. He wanted to transplant it immediately, because he said it would wither and die if left there in the shade for too long. It's true that some percentage of forest seedlings die, but what would happen if we just left this little one alone? Perhaps we can wait to move it until it is a little bigger and stronger. Perhaps it'll be safer there, protected by the trees around it, during the storms of October and November. Had he forgotten he wanted to put a horse in there?

Evelio showed me his first harvested rice plant today. He grabbed a sheet of brown paper from Roger's workshop and laid it on the ground to catch the grains as he carefully stripped them off the stalk. I picked up a few and admired them.

"How to you get rid of the hulls?" I asked.

He told me he needed to find a *pilón,* a hip-high wooden mortar with a heavy, yard-long pestle with which you pound the grains. I've seen hundreds of these old *pilones* around Costa Rica, almost all carved from a single log, usually adorning somebody's patio as an antique. I never knew until now what they were for. He told me that when he was twelve, his mother would send him out to the *pilón* with a bag of unhulled rice to pound for the family dinner. He said it would take him an hour of pounding the thing, then throwing handfuls up in the air so the breeze would blow off the chaff, then pounding some more, and it was hard work. His mother wanted the rice *clean*. "I like that kind of work," he said.

I reminded him that there's an old man selling country tools and cast-iron stoves and other *campesino* items in a run-down shack across from the clinic in Tilarán, and that he might find one there – but he certainly wouldn't want to pay antique prices for something that was a fixture of his childhood. He suspects Rosa's father Pedro still has one at home. I'm sorry I won't get to see this particular operation. It would bring the garden "full circle" – producing the food for the table – in a way that my simple washing of the lettuce and the cucumbers just doesn't do.

We've been having a heat wave, Evelio informs me, another gift of *El Niño*. He gets this information from the television at his mother's house; we don't watch TV and I almost never bother to read the weather in *La Nación*, because it so rarely refers to our part of the country. I haven't checked the thermometer lately either. Apparently, it's only in cold weather, my old nemesis, that I care to know exactly to what degree I am suffering. Though it's obviously hot in the sun, we have yet to turn on a fan in the house, but while dinner was cooking last night it did get hot in the kitchen, so I went out to the stoop to cool off. There wasn't a ripple in the reflection of the lights from the far shore. I leaned against a verandah post and closed my eyes to better feel the relative cool against my skin. Then came the faintest breath – a *whoosh* – of air across the water, and I opened my eyes to see the lights commence a slow-dance on the lake.

A night this warm is rare. In addition to failing to think

about the need to weather-strip around the doors and windows for the cold, we failed to insulate the roof to protect us from the heat. It's a double-roof – recycled plastic tiles over corrugated tin – and the attic is deep. We've never felt the need for insulation before, but it occurs to me that now might be a good time to start thinking about preparing for hotter weather.

On another *mas o menos* morning, Evelio and I talked about his finding work. He knows he needs a change. Even his mother is asking why he seems so sad. "Maybe you should get a job and stop trying to be a farmer," she said to him the other day. I told him I had observed over the year how his spirits rose and fell with the weather and all the other unpredictable conditions and suggested she might have a point. But he went on to complain that the banks won't lend him any money. Only the rich can get money out of the banks, he says. I read in the paper that there's still plenty of money in the system for small growers – even with the recession – but Evelio's problem is that he doesn't fit the profile. He has no land. He has no wife and children who could make up the small family enterprise so favored by state institutions. He's pushing fifty, and he has money in the bank – why should they lend him money if he has savings? The state wants to invest in the young, not in people who are getting on to be pensioners.

I can see why he feels depressed and inclined to believe that the world is treating him unfairly. I tried to help him see how talented and experienced he is, and how his history and his willingness to work hard can be assets, especially on a construction job. Because of the recession, construction is down – *La Nación* describes many of the abandoned projects on the beaches as "ghost towns" – but we do know a builder who's heading off to supervise a large condominium and hotel project, and I suggested Evelio call him.

"If agriculture is so hard on you emotionally, Evelio," I said, "maybe it really makes sense for you to work at something more secure."

I think he heard me, because the next day he told me he'd given the builder a call, only to find the project wouldn't be hiring until December.

"Not to worry." I put my hand on his arm. "I still have a long list of projects for you to do around here."

The fact is, I feel responsible for Evelio. Having given him the opportunity to make an organic garden on our land and having watched him go through all the attendant highs and frustrations, I feel I owe him something. I feel he has a right to expect the best from me, whether it's work, or an empathetic ear, or simple encouragement. It turns out that when you give something to someone, you're also giving to yourself.

Yesterday, a Sunday, when no one was here, I went down to the woodshed-cum-gardening shed to look around. It's another space – like the windsurf center when he was living there – that Evelio has domesticated. He has assembled rough shelves to hold all the paraphernalia to make the organic pesticide – plastic jars, a small scale, the filter from a coffee maker, spray bottles, all lying under a layer of dust. There's a nook for the plastic bags I'd been saving for him from the supermarket vegetable section and stacks of dried lettuce heads and bean pods waiting for their seeds to be shucked. There are two worm-farm boxes still in production. I pried off the covers he's using to keep predators out and turned over the black compost with a small trowel, pleased to see there are still some worms in there. Not a lot, but probably enough to keep the things going with a little care. Along one wall he has carefully hung his hoes and shovels and rakes, and there's a spot on top of some leftover fire bricks for his shoes and rubber boots. Across one corner is stretched a string to which are tied more corn cobs drying. He has cleverly used the husks to tie them up. Over all hovered a sense of desuetude, a faint, earthy smell of loss, and for a moment I felt like crying.

The wind shot out of the north and blew the heat away. We've had more than a week of brilliant, breezy days, and Roger has been happily skidding across the lake behind a sail almost every one of them. This is the kind of weather we'd all like to see go on forever, but the lack of rainfall is already making itself felt in the Pacific lowlands, where the drought has claimed over half the rice crop, and the Ministry of Agriculture is advising cattlemen how to protect their herds. When *El Niño* reigns, there are the inevitable grim photos in the paper of farmers holding up handfuls of desiccated crops and – much more horrible to see – the sharp bony sides of Brahma cattle lying, and dying, in the dust for lack of water and grass. Here in the highlands, Evelio is grateful for the sun to dry his corn, but I haven't asked him about his rice. I suspect he's just going to let it go since, now, even Rosa says, there's not enough of it to be worth all the effort of harvesting.

As the weeds take over, as Nature takes back her own, it becomes harder and harder to find things in the garden. I asked Koki the other day to see if he could spot a young *ayote* for me. With his big rubber boots on and his machete always to hand, it's safer for him to look for things out there. A dietary delicacy for snakes is rats, and rats nibble on seeds. That garden is almost nothing more than a *seed* farm now, and I'm not happy wandering around in it where the high weeds have invaded. We're only ten minutes away from help should any of us be struck by a *terciopelo* (fer-de-lance), but that doesn't mean I'm willing to risk it. I know people who have been bitten, and they experience pain and nerve damage long after the event. I *always* walk – even in the grass Koki has shaved to its roots – with my head down.

I read the other day about a man coming across a long-abandoned farm in the wilderness forest between here and Monteverde. Only the outlines in stone of the old house remained, with a caved-in well, all completely invaded by the ravaging jungle. There were fruit trees, much tangled in vines, and amid the lush growth on one side of the house were some dried corn stalks, still with a few ears on them (all pecked-out by the birds). Agriculture had flourished there once, in the middle of the forest, a self-sustaining family farm. Now just the archeological remains, including some cultivated plants, bore witness to the human lives that had been lived there.

As Nature reclaims Evelio's garden, I wonder if, years from now, under the trees and brush that will have grown back there, a paleontologist will find an ancient beet.

I've often complained about how frustrating it is to try to identify a hawk or falcon or eagle because of the great distances from which you normally see them – and forget owls, because they're nocturnal – so imagine my pleasure at seeing two, close up, on the same day. One, unfortunately, was in a cage, a stunning immature Pacific screech owl that had been orphaned and raised from a chick. Its goldy-buff breast feathers were fluffed with dark vertical streaks, and the poor creature was having trouble keeping its heavily fringed eyes open. I'm guessing that the cage should have been covered during the day, but instead it sat behind a restaurant counter where tourists pay their bills, and I'm sure the owner sees it as an "attraction." Knowing him to care about animals, I'm sure he hopes to release the owl when it's ready to fly. It brings mixed feelings, seeing a baby like that – a rare and beautiful sight, but its survival is far from assured.

Then, as I headed home along the north shore of the lake, on a hairpin curve my eye was drawn to a hawk sunning its spread wings in a dead tree right next to the road. I braked to see him better but dared not stop the car. As I craned to keep him in view as long as I could, he turned his magnificent head to watch me drive by. I kept repeating his markings in my mind all the way home so I wouldn't forget: lead-colored back, white breast, short single-banded tail – the semiplumbeous hawk, according to The Book. What a treat!

On the autumn equinox there are broad, dry leaves accumulating underfoot on the driveway below the compound tree. There's still humidity to soften the edge of the northerly wind, not that clear bite to the air that warns of winter cold. Yesterday, for the first time since April, I went over to the hotel pool late in the afternoon. The water has warmed up nicely with this uninterrupted string of sunny days. I had the place all to myself, except for a curious dragonfly hovering a foot over the water. The temperature was perfect. After my slow laps, I floated in the shallow end and listened to a contrapuntal two-band howler monkey concert in the jungle down the hill. With its view of the lake, the tropical vegetation at one end, the nearby forest and the open sky above, this is truly a heavenly place to swim. I'll try to do this as long as the weather lasts.

Both of my parents died in the month of September, Mom just a few days before 9/11, Dad almost exactly two years later – both of them suddenly, thus sparing my sister and me the heartbreakingly long caregiving so many of our generation have had to face. But in the case of our father, there was another kind of agony.

Just weeks after Mom died, in 2001, Dad started seeing other women. This drove my sister crazy – she was living close by and managing his affairs, and the situation was impossible to ignore – but he was living in a condo building where there were far more widows than widowers. He had never lived alone in his life and, at the age of eighty, he wasn't about to start. And, because he was still a tall, good-looking guy with a decent income, he was actively pursued. He finally settled on an attractive woman in her seventies with one leg, named Carol.

My sister stood tight-lipped through the simple June 2003 ceremony in Dad's apartment ... and got even more annoyed when Dad decided to take Carol to Costa Rica for a September wedding trip, exactly two years after Mom's death. Alison urged me on the phone not to encourage this idea, saying that Dad was getting more and more senile and incontinent, but my feeling was – and Roger shared it – that if Dad wanted to have a last fling, he should be allowed to. Besides, Carol wasn't senile and, even though she was bound to a wheelchair or walker, we figured she could keep things under control.

We met their late flight and took them to the Marriott,

where Carol whispered to me that it had been like traveling with a two-year-old. Dad seemed in good spirits, and as we helped them settle into the room, he knew enough about where he was to order up a double whiskey from room service. We didn't stay to enjoy it with him; we were overnighting in a much cheaper hotel. The next morning, after plowing through a full plate of bacon, sausage, hash-browns, eggs, and half a basket of baked-on-site breads with plenty of butter and jam, my father, who had already had two carotid artery operations, ordered vanilla ice cream with chocolate sauce. I started to protest, but Roger squeezed my arm to shush me.

We had arranged for a friend, a licensed nature guide, to take them down to the Caribbean coast in his supposedly air-conditioned van. Dad had never been to the Caribbean side, and he wanted to see it with his new wife. I had made reservations in a hotel Roger and I had stayed in, so I knew the layout and wasn't too worried. The problem was the fact that the van wasn't air-conditioned, and only a couple of days later Luis Diego called on his cell phone to say they were already on their way back north, three days early. Fortunately, the house I had rented for them nearby was ready, and when they arrived in the late afternoon, everything was in order, including the complimentary bottle of wine offered by their absent hosts. We opened that to have a celebratory glass together, and then I left to run over to our house to pick up the spaghetti sauce and other things for their dinner.

When I got back, Dad was stalking angrily from their bathroom to the one next to the kitchen with a towel wrapped around his waist. The electric shower in his room wasn't working. As accustomed as he was to the Costa Rican milieu, he let this one get to him too much. I was stirring the spaghetti sauce at the stove when I heard the heavy thump.

It has taken me years to figure out why Costa Ricans install bathtub spigots in the showers. It's a frugal culture, and when you buy the showerhead and faucets, the spigot is part of the package, so you install it – nothing should ever go to waste. I threw open the bathroom door to find my father's naked body crumpled on the shower floor, the nape of his neck jammed firmly against the spigot. I hollered his name over and over, but his unmoving eyes told me he was already gone.

It is the longest night in my memory; the details still play through my mind in slow motion. Somehow I had to walk out of that bathroom door and announce to my father's bride that he was dead. She went into hysterics. I made my way to the phone in a daze and called my friend Rosa Emilia, whose husband was the director of the local Red Cross. Then I called Roger. The ambulance with its three attendants arrived within ten minutes, but they pronounced my father dead. Because the Red Cross in Costa Rica is not permitted to transport the dead, and because it was potentially an accident, they were obliged by law to call the police and tack up yellow tape around the bathroom as if to mark a crime scene. This really drove Carol crazy, and she kept trying to ram the yellow tape with her wheelchair. In between these attempts she was pouring herself liberal measures of scotch.

Rosa Emilia and her husband, Roberto, arrived. The maid and the gardener were lurking around the edges of the kitchen, and a few neighbors filed in. An accidental death was a local event worth peeking in on.

When the police showed up there were interrogations all around, and because Carol didn't speak Spanish, I had to interpret for her. A judge had been called to officially pronounce the probable cause of death before the body could be removed, but it was a Friday night, and it took three hours for him to get there. During all this time there seemed to be a hundred people milling around in that house. Finally, the maid pulled out some bread and cheese and made a pot of coffee, while Carol continued to drink, crying intermittently. Roger was sitting helpless in a dark corner of the living room, so I sent him home.

Roberto warned me that after the official pronouncement, they would lift my father's body out of the shower and carry it into the kitchen, where there was room enough on the floor to slide him into a long black plastic bag. As they brought him out, Carol rolled screaming over to him, insisting that she be allowed a final kiss. Even though this little scene was played in English, no one was in any doubt as to her intention, and they held his upper body so that she could lean over to give him a long kiss on the mouth. I couldn't watch. I turned back just as they were maneuvering his limp body into the bag, and then I lost it. Rosa Emilia, who only comes up to my shoulder, wrapped her arms around me and let me sob it out.

Later, after everyone had gone and Carol lay sleepless in her room, I sat on the porch overlooking the dark jungle and the shimmer of the lake, smoking cigarettes and trying to fill the desperate vacuum inside me. It was my fault for encouraging him to come. It was my fault for not checking whether the shower worked. It was all just, just *my fault*.

I lived with this for the six long months it took for the final autopsy report to arrive. I couldn't bear to look at the details – the drawings only reinforced the revulsion I had felt at the sight of his dead naked body. But the results indicated a massive stroke, an instant killer that had thrown him to the shower floor that night, nothing else. The awful burden was lifted, but the heaviness had already worn deep grooves in my heart.

Our father was a charming man with many, many friends. He was a handy fellow and was always fixing things for his neighbors. He loved a good party and could dance and drink with the best of them. He especially loved to tell elaborate shaggy-dog stories. The dark side, the abused side that knew nothing other than to abuse those close to him, was our family secret. But I so well remember the contrast between these two sides of him and how I ached to be loved by the charming one. It was my fault, you see, that I wasn't. All these years after his death, I am still scraping away the guilty residue from the lengths of my bones.

This was the final environmental insult: a man with a gasoline-powered pump spraying the brush with an herbicide (Koki guessed Roundup) right along the fence separating Evelio's garden from the cow-pasture on the other side. I watched from the verandah. There was a breeze. If he turned the corner to spray along the long northeastern side, the stuff would waft right onto the vegetables. I called Koki, but he wasn't within earshot. I called Evelio, and he walked out into the garden and stood, a good 60 feet from where the man was working, folded his arms and stared at him for five minutes.

When I saw him turn to come back toward the house, I called, "Evelio, why didn't you speak to him?"

"I don't want problems with *any*body," he shouted back.

Then I heard him go hollering for Koki. So *tico,* I said to myself, exasperated. Sometimes this non-confrontational culture really gets me.

Minutes later Koki came rushing up, and I explained that I wanted him to find out who had ordered the man to spray, and to ask him to please stay well away from our fenceline. Koki went over to speak to him, and when he came back he reported that the man had said, essentially, "I just work here, Bud, talk to my boss." So I asked Koki to call our neighbor to get her to tell the man to respect our crops. He spoke to her husband, instead, who is much more reasonable, and he authorized Koki to go back out into the field to tell the man his boss had said to stay ten feet away from the line. Done. But not saved.

When I looked at Evelio, who was head-down

varnishing a door, I started to say, "Evelio, why didn't ...?" and he looked up, eyes flashing anger, and said that he didn't trust himself to have a conversation with the guy without losing his temper.

I understood. There are depredations, violations, expressions of disrespect that just take one from calm to rage in a nanosecond with no elevating stages in between. I have felt rage like that, mostly when I've seen people willfully and arrogantly breaking environmental law, and I know that this kind of anger, over time, can kill you. You have to learn to walk away, let it go, find calmer ways of negotiating solutions. You read in the paper about *campesinos* getting killed by machetes every year, always over some property issue, more and more frequently, of late, over water. Evelio knew that a face-to-face confrontation with an armed man was dangerous, especially given his own inability to control his feelings. I admire this kind of self-understanding.

The other question is, of course, how to protect an organic plot of ground from environmental depredations that originate *outside* it? I won't even get into the subject of wind-borne seed from genetically modified crops – that is a huge issue and, fortunately for us, right on this farm, it isn't a problem. That field upwind of us is too steep to plant. It has repeatedly tried to reforest itself in the years we have been here, and men keep slashing it down with machetes to make room for the cows. This is the first time I've seen spray. It must be expensive. The result will surely be hideous. I wonder how many deer will sicken or die from eating this newly poisoned vegetation. The cattleman isn't thinking about these things.

Several days later, Evelio took me on a tour of the damage: tomato plants, carrot tops, the sensitive cilantro stalks, all curled and bent over, stricken as if from some terrible internal blight. On the other side of the fence, the leaves on the brush were wilted and starting to brown. Evelio said it would be a month or two before the cattleman lets his herd back into the field. If we had a big crop here, he explained, we could go to the law and seek some redress, but for the few things still left growing – or rather, dying – here, we have no claim. He said he would check the trees. It's illegal to kill a tree. And the soil, according to international organic standards, will have to wait another three years before we can call anything grown here organic again. Except for the rice growing out of the way of the wind, the garden is dead.

For a couple of days, Evelio's been noisily using the table saw and the drill downstairs, and I've seen Fortuna hauling off tasty bits of bamboo to chew on. It turns out to be his *máquina*, or rice-harvesting frame. When I went out to the field to watch this operation this morning, I was impressed by the simple beauty of the thing: four three-inch-diameter bamboo uprights held together in a rough three-foot-square by four lateral pieces, a couple of angles to keep it rigid, with a lattice of smaller bamboo stalks each about an inch apart, lashed to the top of the frame with plastic string.

"All natural," he said, beaming.

He showed me the *cuchillo de os*, a small, curved serrated blade, all made by *hand*. He got it from a cousin who had spent a lifetime harvesting rice. Harvesting is a simple, back-breaking job: a swift backwards cut at the base of the rice stalks, tossing them to one side as you work. Then the stalks are gathered into sheaves and whacked against the frame, so that the grains fall through the lattice onto a large plastic sheet below. Then, as with everything else in this country, they're left out in the sun to dry until it's time to thresh them in the *pilón*. Evelio says he has to get the rice in soon, because the grackles are just waiting for him to get out of the way. They can strip hectares of rice in a day.

I understand now that it's in part the rituals of this traditional agriculture that have enchanted Evelio so. It's not just the smell of the earth, or even eating what he grows, but the entire process, from turning over the ground to drying and threshing the crop to painstakingly saving the seed for next time – including the manufacture from scratch of many of the tools and materials he needs – that he loves to reenact. It's a *play* I have been watching all year, a drama, with Evelio, the hero *Agricultor,* buffeted by the Wind and the Weather in the key supporting roles, and challenged by Leafcutter Ants and Agri-chemicals in the walk-on parts. It's a drama over 10,000 years old. I have wondered in recent months how farmers keep at it. On a small scale, at the level of immediate survival, it's almost pure gamble. It has to be a sense of participating in something grand and important and dignified, a Herculean task that is never done, that makes them work so hard against such huge odds.

At sunset on the last day of the month, the sky is layered with lavender, and small clouds chug across the lake like puffs of smoke from a steam engine. A huge salmon-pink tower of cumulus explodes into the upper atmosphere, where the winds push its head over into the shape of a massive anvil. An ovoid translucent moon slips out from behind the mist lying on the hills, casting its pink light over the nacreous surface of the lake.

Down in the lower reaches of the Quebrada Bullicioso, the tree frogs are ululating an accompaniment to the cicadas. Up on the Continental Divide, a yipping pack of coyotes is getting ready for its nightly hunt. A lone monkey barks briefly in the trees behind the house.

It's clear to me now that what you get out of a garden may not be directly related to what you put *into* it. What was the total yield? Evelio will always feel that he didn't harvest enough. I got a couple ears of Hawaiian sweet corn, thirty radishes, five zucchini, fifteen cucumbers, an equal number of tiny sweet peppers, a few handfuls of carrots, three months' worth of lettuce, a deeper sense of my connection to the earth, and one friend.

I can't feel too bad about the loss of Evelio's garden, because I know he will find another.

As for my own – seemingly so chaotically planted and haphazardly tended over a long life – perhaps, finally, I am beginning to enjoy its fruits. Evelio has helped me to see that, in this magical place called Earth, it is given to us to understand and know ourselves. It is given to us to grow, love and move on.

Epilogue
Ten Years Later

Interamericana Norte: Driving north from San José, one now emerges from the cathedral of new green growth on the overhanging limbs of the old guanacaste trees to a scarred moonscape of brown dirt and dust churned up by toy-sized earth movers on either side of the right of way. All the trees in the way long have been cut down, but in a small ironic twist, the road workers have staked flag posts (made of tree limbs) along both sides of the road to keep us from wandering off the cliff into the construction zone. Many of these have started to sprout new green growth. No matter how hard we try, we can't stop the Inevitable. The resulting four-lane highway will cut travel time to San José, just as the new highway from Cañas to Liberia has done the same, but it's a man-made thing in the dry tropical forest, and I miss the trees.

We had to fire Koki. We had grown used to his annual two-week binges, and things didn't fall apart too much during his absences. Sometimes we hired a dayworker or two. But finally, he was out for six weeks, "sleeping like a dog in the street," according to his mother. I told her to tell him to get over here *pronto,* or he'd lose his job. That worked. I had explored options with AA in Tilarán. There was a rehab house in San José, a two-week program, and I told Koki he could go and we'd pay for it, but the first time he fell off the wagon after that, he was fired. Period. He came back a "changed man," he said, but it wasn't a year later that he went off again. I drew up the necessary papers for him to sign (the labor law is very strict about this process), which he did, and we hired the young man who had been replacing him during his absence: Manuel, who has been a dream to work with. Thoughtful, respectful, he thinks ahead about one's needs. He also loves dogs. Rosa is still with me – twenty years now we have been together – and I was shocked to discover that she is now fifty-nine and anticipating her retirement. "Not until I'm dead," I shrieked at her, and she laughed. We'll see who goes first.

We never knew how old Fortuna was when she was thrust upon us by our vet friend Eric. And I can't fix the number of years she was with us beyond ten; I never keep track of dates like that, as animals come and go. She was certainly a *personage* in our lives all that time, and as she started to fail and multiple trips to the vet identified nothing specific we could treat beyond pain, we worried about when we should put her down. She still followed Manuel about his rounds, albeit more slowly, and he was reluctant, as most Costa Ricans are, to tell us she was ready to go. So we delayed, until one day our dear old Fortuna wandered off into the forest alone and never came back. Manuel found her a couple of days later, and he buried her in the pet cemetery. It felt like the end of an era to lose her so unceremoniously like that.

Moving: After four years (or was it six?) on the market, the house and land finally found just the right buyer, although at a price a little more than half that suggested by the first realtor to visit so many years ago. Over the years we lowered the price in small increments to no avail. And, as a consequence of the 2008 recession and my lousy decision making with regard to investments, I found myself perched on the abyss of running out of money to keep our workers going and the taxes paid, when the miracle buyers showed up for whom the property was perfect. This involved some significant mourning on my part – although, thank God, my sister was here to absorb my sobs after the closing. "Breathe deeply," she kept saying, strong arms holding me tight against her, and she set up a breathing rhythm I could eventually follow in order to shut down the contractions of my chest. Whatever could I have done without her loving self?

Yet another contraction: with increasing delight, I have been giving things away. Roger has built yet another new room onto "the little house," into which he moved at my urging when I felt there were too many reasons for our not living together anymore (much as our essential love has held strong), a space perfect for the results of my mother's antique-hunting sorties in the Bucks County, Pennsylvania of the sixties with her then-lover. There's something about these acquisitions I find it hard to part with. They represent to me a compensation for her pain. So, Roger will keep them until (or if) I ever have room for them again.

There's a small bungalow on a private farm, address: *Peninsula No One, 700 meters northwest of the Tronadora High school, Tilarán, Guanacaste.* I have to open and close the main farm gate every time I want to go anywhere, and I continue to compare myself to what I was at fifty in similar circumstances – downsizing – and find myself complaining that a woman in her seventies shouldn't have to live with such inconveniences. I am promised that an automatic gate is in the owner's plans. After I had finally rid myself of all the boxes and arranged several clearly identifiable living spaces, I invited Roger over to have a look, and his first remark was, "It looks like a junk shop!" I did not find this comforting, but then he's never been a paragon of tact.

It's another El Niño year. I read in the paper the other day they're predicting a nine-month drought on the Pacific side. This affects *all* countries on the Pacific side of the Americas, some to a lesser degree than others, but the resulting fires, deaths from heat stroke, scrambles to provide water for crops and for people to drink, the cattle here dying in the dust of the Guanacaste Plain. It's sad to contemplate that climate change is changing so many lives for the worse. Here the lake is as low as we've seen it, and ICE is buying electricity from the Central American grid rather than fire up its own bunker plants. Of course, the grid is mostly supplied by bunker, too.

Happily, Evelio has continued to find new organic gardens, first for an old hippie in Tronadora, who, after several years, lost patience with Evelio's slow pace, and then, through Roger, a wealthy patron in Sabalito, who has him building raised beds all over his lawn and filling them with organic vegetables. Roger is also finding him other little projects, so every time I see Evelio it's with a hug and a happy face. I am glad that he seems finally to have found his niche – and Roger is building him a little house! Down by his gate where the old cow shed was, a tiny place tucked right up against the jungle of the *quebrada,* it will suit Evelio perfectly, and serve Roger as a guardhouse in the bargain.

Roger has been super busy supervising building projects, one leading to the next, and he too (although deaf as a post) seems happily busy and content living on his own. If I need anything, he helps, and vice versa. It's a friendly arrangement all around, and I, too, in my third age, am settling happily into my little bungalow down near the lake, with plenty of green all around, another foundling cat, monkeys hollering Reveille and Taps, and a cotillion of frogs singing me to sleep through the May nights. Life is good.

SSH
June, 2019

Acknowledgments

A few passages in this book are adapted from pieces first published in *The Tico Times,* Costa Rica's first English-language weekly; the *Oasis Journal 2014; Sky Island Journal;* and on the blogs of livingabroadincostarica.com and writingfromtheheart.net.

Special thanks to my birdwatching sister, Alison Shaw, for her patience and persistence in identifying most of the birds included here.

For the Naturalist
Birds Identified on Our Farm

American Swallow-tailed
Kite
Ant Shrike
Baltimore Oriole
(migrating)
Black Hawk
Black & White Warbler
Black Vulture
Black-cheeked
Woodpecker
Black-throated Trogon
Blue and White Swallow
Blue-black Grassquit
Blue-crowned Manakin
Blue-crowned Motmot
Blue Dacnis
Blue-gray Tanager
Boat-billed Flycatcher
Bronzed Cowbird
Brown Jay
Brown-crested Flycatcher
Buff-throated Saltator
Cattle Egret
Cinnamon
Hummingbird
Clay-colored Robin
Collared Aracari
Crested Guan
Crimson-fronted

Parakeet
Dusky Nightjar
Golden-hooded Tanager
Gray-capped Flycatcher
Gray-headed Chachalaca
Gray-necked Wood-rail
Great Kiskadee
Great-tailed Grackle
Green Hermit
Groove-billed Ani
Hepatic Tanager
Hoffman's Woodpecker
House Wren
Keel-billed Toucan
Laughing Falcon
Lesser Goldfinch
Lineated Woodpecker
Little Hermit
Long-tailed Manakin
Masked Tityra
Montezuma Oropéndola
Nicaraguan Grackle
Northern Jacana
Nutting's Flycatcher
Pale-vented Pigeon
Philadelphia Vireo
Plain Chachalaca
Red-legged
Honeycreeper

Red-lored Parrot
Ruddy Quail-Dove
Rufous-and-white Wren
Scarlet Tanager
(migrating)
Scarlet-rumped Tanager
Scrub Euphonia
Squirrel Cuckoo
Streaked-headed
Woodcreeper
Sulphur-bellied
Flycatcher
Swainson's Thrush
Turkey Vulture
White- winged Dove
White-collared Manakin
White-collared Seedeater
White-necked Jacobin
White-ringed Flycatcher
White-throated Magpie-
Jay
White-winged Tanager
Wood Stork
Yellow Warbler
Yellow-bellied Elaenia
Yellow-bellied Flycatcher
Yellow-bellied Sapsucker
Yellow-billed Cacique
Yellow-faced Grasquit
Yellow-headed Caracara
Yellow-throated
Euphonia*

Flora and Fauna

This is only a partial list of species mentioned in the text, as the local Spanish name for a species is not to be found online or in my reference books. Here I offer the scientific names where I have been able to find them.

Armadillo,
Dasypus novemcinctus
Banana, *Musa acuminata*
Bird of Paradise,
Stretlitzia reginae
Carablanca,
Cebus capucinus
Cedro, *Cedreda odorata*
Ceiba, *Ceiba pentandra*
Cicada, Sundown,
Fidicina mannifera
Coral snake,
Micrurus nigrocinctus
Corteza Amarillo,
Tabebuia ochracea
Coyote, *Canis latrans*
Crocodile,
Crocodylus acutus
Deer, White-tailed,
Odocoileus virginianus
Estrella grass,
Cynodon nlemfuensis
Eucalyptus,
Eucalyptus deglupta
Eyelash viper,
Bothrops schiegelii

Fig, *Ficus*
Fer de lance,
Bothrops asper
Fire ant,
Solenopsis invicta
Ginger,
Alpinia purpurata
Golden shower tree,
Cassia fistula
Guanacaste,
Enterolobium cyclocarpin
Guanábana,
Annona muricata
Guanijiquil, *Inga vera*
Guachipelín,
Diphysa americana
Guava, *Psidium guajava*
Güitite,
Acnistus arborescens
Gumbo Limbo,
Bursera simaruba
Heliconias:
Heliconia latispatha
Heliconia pogonantha
Higuerón,
Ficus costaricana

Honduran white bat,
Ectophylla alba
Impatiens,
Impatiens walleriana
Itabo,
Yucca guatemalensis
Jamaican fruit-eating
bat, *Artibeus*
jamaicensis
Jocote,
Spondias purpurea
Laurel, *Cordia alliodora*
Leaf-cutter ant,
Atta cephalotes
Lengua de vaca,
Conostegia xalapensis
Madero Negro,
Gliricidia sepium
Maracuyá,
Passiflora ligularis
Monkey, Mantled Howler,
Alouatta palliata
Monkey, White-faced,
Cebus capucinus
Muñeco,
Cordia collococca L.
Murciélago,
Artibeus jamaicensis
Orchid tree,
Bauhinia variegata

Owl butterfly,
Caligo memnon
Palm viper,
Bothriecis schlegelii
Papaya, *Carica papaya*
Pejibaye,
Bactris gasipaes
Pineapple,
Ananas comosus
Rhinoceros beetle,
Megasoma elephas
Roble de Sabana,
Tabebuia rosea
Sea Snake, Pelagic,
Pelamis platurus
Sloth, Two-toed,
Choloepus hoffmanni
Strangler Fig,
Ficus aurea
Squirrel, Deppe's,
Sciurus deppei
Terciopelo,
Bothrops asper
Uruca,
Trichilia bahanensis
Yesterday-today-and
tomorrow, *Brunfelsia*
grandiflora
Zapote, *Pouteria sapota*

Recommended Reading

Allen, William, *The Green Phoenix: Restoring the Tropical Forests of Guanacaste, Costa Rica,* Oxford University Press, 2001

Alvarado, Guillermo, *Costa Rica: Land of Volcanoes,* Gallo Pinto Press, 1993

Bernhardt, Ed, *The Costa Rican Organic Home Gardening Guide,* New Dawn Center, 2003

Biesanz, Mavis, Richard Biesanz, and Karen Zubris Biesanz, *The Ticos: Culture and Social Change in Costa Rica,* Lynne Rienner Publishers, Inc., 1999

Chapman, Peter, *Bananas: How the United Fruit Company Shaped the World,* Canongate Books, Ltd., 2007

Forsyth, Adrian & Miyata, Ken, *Tropical Nature: Life and Death in the Rain Forests of Central and South America,* Simon & Schuster, 1984

Janzen, Daniel H., et. al, *Costa Rican Natural History,* University of Chicago Press, 1983

Parsons, Kimberly, Adrian Colesberry & Brass McLean, *Costa Rica: The Last Country the Gods Made,* Sky House Publishers, 1993

Reid, Fiona A., *A Field Guide to the Mammals of Central America and Southeast Mexico,* Oxford University Press, 1997

Skutch, Alexander F., *A Naturalist on a Tropical Farm,* University of California Press, 1980

Stiles, F. Gary & Alexander F. Skutch, *A Guide to the Birds of Costa Rica,* Cornell University Press, 1989

Stuart, Josephine, *Butterfly in the City: A Good Life in Costa Rica,* Litografía e Imprente LIL ,S.A., 2006

Van Rheenen, Erin, *Living Abroad in Costa Rica,* Fifth Edition, Avalon Travel Publishing, 2017

Zuchowski, Willow, *A Guide to Tropical Plants of Costa Rica,* Distribuidores Zona Tropical, S.A., 2005

Glossary

Agricultor: dignified word for farmer
Aguacero: heavy rainfall
Arroz: rice
Artisanal: artisan
Asco: disgusting or revolting thing
Bicho: bug, beast
Bueno: good, okay
Bullicioso: tumultuous, noisy
Campesino: rural dweller
Campo: countryside
Cantón: county
Cariño: affection, tenderness
Catastro: official land registry
Cochinada: dirt, filth, a mess
Colón: currency of Costa Rica
Confianza: confidence, trust
Criadero: breeding place
Criollo: native
Cuchillo: knife
De ninguna manera: no way
Desequilibrado: unbalanced,
Desvío: detour
Elote: ear of corn
Excursión: outing
Feo: ugly
Finca: farm
Frijol tapado: method of planting beans protected by
  scrub
Fútbol: soccer
Guaro: liquor made from sugar cane, also generic locally
  for liquor

Guitarreo: strumming (wasps' nest)
Hielo: ice
Las Pintas: first 12 days of January that predict the
    weather for the next 12 months
Llovizna: misty rain
Malcriado: badly raised or behaved
Mandarino: tangerine tree
Máquina: machine, aparatus
Más o menos: more or less
Más tranquila: more peaceful
Matapalo: tree-killer, local name for strangler fig
Medio-medio: neither this nor that
Meseta: plateau
Metate: corn-grinding stone
Montaña: mountain, scrubland or forest
Muy bien: very well
No vale la pena: it's not worth it
Orgánico: organic
Patrona: female employer
Pelo de gato: cat fur or misty rain
Pensión alimenticia: alimony
Permiso: permission
Pilón, large, wooden mortar for hulling rice
Primario: primary, first
Producto: product
Pulpería: corner store
Pura vida: pure life, never better
Quebrada: gorge, ravine
Rancheras: romantic Mexican songs
Remedio: remedy
Rico: rich, delicious
Ropa: clothes
Sarán: nursery cloth
Súper: short for *supermercado*, supermarket
Tamal: traditional Latin American Christmas food
Taxi carga: light truck hired for cargo
Temblor: seismic tremor

Tico: affectionate term for Costa Rican
Tierno: fresh, tender, as vegetables
Trámite: paperwork, red tape
Upe: anybody home? open the door
Vamos a ver: we'll see
Veranillo de San Juan: little summer of St. John, a brief
  dry spell in the rainy season
Zompopa: leaf-cutter ant
Zopilote: vulture

About Atmosphere Press

Atmosphere Press is an independent, full-service publisher for books in genres ranging from nonfiction to fiction to poetry, with a special emphasis on being an author-friendly approach to the challenges of getting a book into the world. Learn more about what we do at atmospherepress.com.

We encourage you to check out some of Atmosphere's latest releases, which are available at Amazon.com and via order from your local bookstore:

Young Yogi and the Mind Monsters, an illustrated retelling of Patanjali by Sonja Radvila
Difficulty Swallowing, essays by Kym Cunningham
Come Kill Me!, short stories by Mackinley Greenlaw
The Unexpected Aneurysm of the Potato Blossom Queen, short stories by Garrett Socol
Gathered, a novel by Kurt Hansen
Interviews from the Last Days, sci-fi poetry by Christina Loraine
Unorthodoxy, a novel by Joshua A.H. Harris
the oneness of Reality, poetry by Brock Mehler
Frank, a novel by Gina DeNicola
Drop Dead Red, poetry by Elizabeth Carmer
Aging Without Grace, poetry by Sandra Fox Murphy
A User Guide to the Unconscious Mind, nonfiction by Tatiana Lukyanova
To the Next Step: Your Guide from High School and College to The Real World, nonfiction by Kyle Grappone
The George Stories, a novel by Christopher Gould
No Home Like a Raft, poetry by Martin Jon Porter

Mere Being, poetry by Barry D. Amis

Breathing New Life: Finding Happiness after Tragedy, nonfiction by Bunny Leach

Mandated Happiness, a novel by Clayton Tucker

The Third Door, a novel by Jim Williams

The Yoga of Strength, a novel by Andrew Marc Rowe

They are Almost Invisible, poetry by Elizabeth Carmer

Let the Little Birds Sing, a novel by Sandra Fox Murphy

Auroras over Acadia, poetry by Paul Liebow

Channel: How to be a Clear Channel for Inspiration by Listening, Enjoying, and Trusting Your Intuition, nonfiction by Jessica Ang

Love Your Vibe: Using the Power of Sound to Take Command of Your Life, nonfiction by Matt Omo

Transcendence, poetry and images by Vincent Bahar Towliat

Leaving the Ladder: An Ex-Corporate Girl's Guide from the Rat Race to Fulfilment, nonfiction by Lynda Bayada

Adrift, poems by Kristy Peloquin

Letting Nicki Go: A Mother's Journey through Her Daughter's Cancer, nonfiction by Bunny Leach

Time Do Not Stop, poems by William Guest

Dear Old Dogs, a novella by Gwen Head

How Not to Sell: A Sales Survival Guide, nonfiction by Rashad Daoudi

Ghost Sentence, poems by Mary Flanagan

What Outlives Us, poems by Larry Levy

Winter Park, a novel by Graham Guest

That Beautiful Season, a novel by Sandra Fox Murphy

What I Cannot Abandon, poems by William Guest

All the Dead Are Holy, poems by Larry Levy

About the Author

Sandra Shaw Homer has lived in Costa Rica for 29 years, where she has taught languages and worked as an interpreter/translator and environmental activist. In addition to a column in the local press, her creative nonfiction, fiction and poetry have appeared in a variety of print and online literary and travel journals, as well as on her own blog, writingfromtheheart.net. Her travel memoir, *Letters from the Pacific: 49 Days on a Cargo Ship*, received excellent Kirkus and Publishers Weekly reviews. Go to https://www.facebook.com/writingfromtheheart.net/ ?ref=bookmarks for more information.

CPSIA information can be obtained
at www.ICGtesting.com
Printed in the USA
FFHW021509071019
55427546-61190FF